The "A" Word: Autism
A Guidebook and Memoir

Michelle Rosenblum, MS, MSed

DEDICATION

For Joshua and Amalia – I love you always.

CONTENTS

FOREWARD

The "A" word, Autism used to roll off my tongue with great ease prior to being married and having an autistic child of my own. I worked with autistic children and fancied myself an expert. How laughable that is now, looking back.

For the first two years after my beautiful boy's diagnosis, I couldn't even speak, what I called, "The A WORD".…. It felt like a swear word, a curse you hear in Harry Potter books, a death sentence, another word for HELL, it was the worst of words, and I avoided it vehemently. I say this to you now, the potential parent, grandparent or just interested reader, as it deeply conveys the pain and denial that parents feel when given the dreaded diagnosis of "Autism".

To address this further and really imprint this message to you, please consider that I personally worked with Autistic children, prior to my son's diagnosis. The "A" word was part of my vernacular, until it hit me too closely.

The good news, and reason I am writing this book, is that I can now speak the dreaded "A" word, laugh about my son's idiosyncrasies, feel Proud of having my son, and I wouldn't change a thing about him, even if presented with a magic button. I have embraced Autism, and my hope is that through reading these pages, you will find promise, beauty, cathartic tears, laughter, wisdom and joy.

Autism is not the death sentence I had believed it would be. Instead, it has taught me to be an excessively patient person, accepting of how things are, non-controlling, did I mention patient? And most importantly, my perfect boy Joshua, has taught me how to truly love a person unconditionally, which I feel is the greatest gift of all.

To all of you out there, please know that it will get better in time, and though it's quite a roller-coaster ride you have gotten on, you will eventually learn to ride it with ease.

Many Blessings,

Michelle Rosenblum MS, MSed

THE DIAGNOSIS

My diagnosis for Joshua was not an uncommon one... We were in the doctor's office, and he looked at me after observing Josh for awhile and said, "So, when did you find out he was Autistic?" WHAT? I was in shock and felt like I was just run-over by a bulldozer. I was completely speechless, numb, but on the border-line of crying. From the look on my face, he quickly assessed that it was in fact the first time I had heard anyone call my little darling, the dreaded, "A" word, Autistic. "Oh, um, I'm sorry... you didn't know he had autism?"

I guess there really is no good way to tell a parent that their child has a developmental disorder, but this was how I learned, alone with my son in that office room, next to a brilliantly intelligent doctor who was quite the clinician, but more scientist than warm and fuzzy Pediatrician.

I remember somehow leaving the office, getting Josh into the car seat and crying and crying. Josh fortunately and unfortunately... wasn't much interested or bothered by my tears, as at that time in his life, he wasn't much connected. He was there, but not entirely there...

And though that day, and the next three days were the toughest most heart-shattering, heart-wrenching, basically, most awful days of my entire life, they were also an inspired beginning. They were the beginning of our journey through the dreaded dark forest of Autism, to the light of the forest's other edge. My new motivation was to cut through the trees, swing over the swamps and get us to the other side, as fast as I could. As fast as God would let me.

I recall and contrast those dark days, years later as Josh decided to entertain us all with a medley of songs, mostly intelligible due to the melody, not necessarily his words. He lined up four chairs, and stood very proudly, and in an uncharacteristically shy manner as well. He sang and sang with a huge smile on his face, and then sang some more. He pointed to his eyes and said, "Eyes", his ears and named them appropriately as well. This feat seemed impossible only a year prior. Every small step feels like a huge leap, and I have learned to concentrate my mind on these steps, rather than what's missing, and that has made all of the difference.

Don't get me wrong. I wasn't always so grateful and gracious. Determined and cluelessly privileged was how I lived the first twenty-five years of my life. At the very naive and spoiled age of twenty two, I had the realization as I was nearing college graduation that I had in fact completed every course on the Theatre Arts-Oral Interpretation curriculum, as well as every class in my psychology minor. But I honestly hadn't given a second thought as to what I would do next. I had no idea why I was getting those degrees, but for sheer interest in the subjects.

Sorry mom and dad and thanks for funding my search for knowledge. And so as I walked by the theatre arts message board one day at beautiful Eastern Michigan University, a flyer that was practically glowing off the board caught my attention. It said, "AMDA" (American Musical and Dramatic Academy) and New York City, and I was sold. In that one moment my path had been made abundantly clear. I had discovered what I must do next, so I applied to AMDA, flew out to audition, won a partial scholarship into the Musical Theatre program, and moved to New York six months later after my parents acquiesced to my pleas for more funding. What else is a girl to do I remember thinking. Just keep getting degrees and eventually meet mister right. Boy was I in for a ride...

Show Business was not a foreign business to me. Though my mom was a full time mother to myself and my three younger siblings, we would often not see her or my father on the week-end evenings. Our kind but lactose intolerant sitter would come over, and my younger sister would follow her around with air freshener spraying it as she walked by. I remember one time our favorite sitter was unavailable and we didn't really care for the person who took her place. I devised a payback plan, one that I hoped would discourage her from ever returning. Not very nice, and in retrospect, I'm very grateful the woman didn't have a heart attack and drop dead on the spot. She was not young, in fact elderly would be a better description. At midnight I turned every speaker in every room in our home up to full volume, found my Michael Jackson cassette tape, cued it to Vincent Price laughing at the end of Thriller, and let it rip! Needless to say, Mrs. Meanie didn't return.

My mom's career was flourishing as a singer and television personality, even guest starring on shows such as "The Ed Sullivan Show", and Jimmy Durante's television hour. When she started having us, she semi-retired and she and my dad had a wedding band. Her stage name is Vickie Carroll. She was raised French Catholic, but that didn't last. Once she met my father Sheldon Rott, an Orthodox Jewish raised musician and record promoter for the Beatles, their love at first sight passion sealed the deal, and she converted to Judaism. I was the lucky recipient of two very different sets of grand-parents, (as well as two sets of Holiday presents) ear to prejudice from people mistaking me for Christian, and others thinking I was Jewish. Perhaps in defiance, or I'd like to think in search of truth, I became a practicing Buddhist for ten years. Got tired of meditating though and gave that up too.

Prior to mom marrying dad, she too had a stint in New York. Her stories however were semi-horror stories that helped me to keep my guard up. She had to stay in ratty cheap hotels that weren't even safe. I however started my excursion through Manhattan in the safer and by New York standards, more luxurious Upper West Side vicinity at a building called the Esplanade, an old folks home who offered some rooms to AMDA for their students. Yep, I felt safe there at 74th and West End Avenue surrounded by nice old ladies and gentlemen. And, I grew to love the Upper West Side of New York dearly, but I just wasn't enjoying my musical theatre training. Dance class for me became more of a comical outlet as I tried raising my leg above the bar in ballet and wound up swinging on it like a monkey instead. I just simply felt out of place, but determined to see it through, until the end of the semester at least.

Quitting my musical theatre program was an option, and after my semester ended, I did just that. Yet, after doing a few off-Broadway shows post-AMDA, I just felt lost. The spark I had for performing didn't return. I was just another small fish in a huge ocean of super talented people, most working as waiters and waitresses, something I'd always wanted to do in fantasy, but not really in reality. In Michigan I was singing the National Anthem at Piston's games in front of 60,000 people, recording commercials and living a cushy lifestyle. In New York, the only reason I would even get a part after spending my time at a day long cattle call, was because I would tell the directors, "Look, you just saw about 1000 people today. Most of them are super talented and by now you probably don't remember any of them. You heard me sing and I can do the job. I'm always on time, and a hard worker. Give me a chance please." And so they often did, but I just didn't feel I was doing what I was truly meant to do, despite my successful determination.

This determination I speak of is what you will also need on your autism jungle ride, and it is what has served me tremendously as Joshie's mom. I realized at age twenty-three that it wasn't important for me to become the next Barbra Streisand anymore. Other paths started speaking to me. My minor in psychology was not by chance. I was very interested in how the mind works, why people act as they do, and I have always wanted to help people, so I decided that a master's degree in teaching would be my next appropriate move. Retiring my audition hopping and backstage magazine subscription were easy to do. Quitting that life was right for me. However, twenty years later, quitting on Josh is not. You may have days that you feel like throwing the towel in. That is completely normal. It's what you do with it that counts. I will never give up on my son, and I hope that you too feel the same way about your child of the spectrum. Chances are that you will know someone who is suffering with Autism if you don't already. The numbers according to the Center for Disease Controls 2014 study have gone up yet again. 1 in 68 children are now being diagnosed with Autism. 1 in 42 are boys. This is a 30 percent rise in only two years.

CHOICES

We have not had forward motion each day of this journey. In fact, most of it felt like a crawl through quick-sand. There is a saying in the autism world, "Three steps backward before a major improvement occurs". What I didn't remember was that sometimes those steps consisted of really tough Weeks, not days, weeks... Still, moments occur that make those quick sand weeks feel a lot less difficult than they really were.

So, what did we do to help Joshie become so successful? And what is success when you have a child diagnosed with Autism? For me, I decided when he was two years old, that success consisted of two words, "Contentment and Ability". What then would help my sweetie to feel capable and empowered in this world, as well as content? I have never been the kind of mom who strives for her children to become honor students, and if my daughter Amalia, who is not Autistic became an honor student, I'd be happy for her, IF she was happy. No, my goals were more simplistic. Two major things popped into my mind at that time in his toddler life. I wanted him to be able to enjoy connection with people and to be potty trained. One psychological and one practical goal.

It just so happened that we were living in a sensory nightmare city, a wonderful city, but a traffic filled, siren ringing sensory screaming city, called Manhattan. I met my husband Ira at HMV record store at 72nd and Broadway on that very island. I was perusing the musical theatre section and a six foot tall handsome man with several earrings in both ears, and several necklaces approached me. I was always more interested in clean cut looking guys, and I thought nothing of him though he did have a nice square jaw bone I remember thinking.. He asked me if I needed help finding anything. He was at that time the World Music Buyer at HMV. I declined his aid, and then he decided to ask me out. However, he didn't say when or where, and as we continued to talk, we got away from the date discussion and I eventually just left.

Six months later I was in the store looking for one musical CD or another during my post AMDA audition phase, needing new material for auditions. Ira remembered me as I browsed the section, approached and said, "So, where have you been? We still have that date..." I thought it was ridiculously funny that he remembered and approached me like that. He then said that he had tickets to a Baaba Maal concert the next evening, and would I like to go? Well, I do like African music, so I said yes. Most of that evening was awful. He brought his friend from work, James who had a voice-emodulation disorder, practically screaming everything he said, and the two of them talk-screamed shop the entire time. I told him that I was going to have to leave as I lied and said I had a headache. Ira didn't seem to care much and his constant chatter left me exhausted, so I started to leave after thanking him. He then grabbed me and kissed me. I was completely shocked, and somewhat dizzy after that kiss, so when he called me the next week, I decided to see him again, and the rest is history. We married in November of 2000, six years after we met. Amalia was born in 2004, and Joshie in 2005.

Two years after Joshua's birth we left New York for a quieter ambience and more space in my home state of Michigan. Joshua's sensory overload in Malls or stadiums or even restaurants at that young stage of his life, was so overpowering, that we rarely visited such places. Staying in New York was not an option. No amount of desensitization training to his environment would have worked. Just walking to the grocery store was painful to him. There were so many sensory obstacles in the city. Of course, too much noise overwhelmed him, such as the traffic of cars, people screaming to each other from across the street, or the dreaded fire truck racing by. It was also at times, too hot having to go out in the August heat or too cold in the dead of winter, and driving places was not an option in the city. Now that we are in a more rural, suburban environment he is far happier. Though, I still see him cover his ears in pain when an ambulance goes by, even when we are indoors. No, New York was not an option.

So we moved to Michigan and the first thing we did was to contact the city school district and ask about special needs services and evaluations. They will evaluate your child, at no cost to you. If they find he or she has some kind of impairment, then an IEP (Individual Educational Plan) meeting will be called and they will explain the specific services that they can offer to your family.

You always have the option of not agreeing to enroll your child. A lot of people are afraid of the stigma that their child will bare if in a special needs class. I was one of them, so I understand completely. But let me put it like this. If your kid is on the spectrum, kids will know, whether they're enrolled or not... And doesn't it make more sense to get them help, than to just let them continue unassisted and at the mercy of school kids? I thought so, and oh how glad I am that I followed through and left fear at the door.

Joshua entered the Autism school program, also known as the AI program in our district, and because of it, he did get potty trained. A very high percentage of Autistic spectrum kids never learn to use the bathroom themselves. Was it easy to potty train him? NO WAY. Would it have been possible to do so without the support of the early intervention team at the school he attended? Maybe, but maybe not. I was an expert or so I thought, and had worked with the special needs population prior to having my own angel on the spectrum, but I still needed much support. It's a vastly different experience working with children from nine to five, and then living your own life after the day is done, not "taking your work home". I have learned so very much more as Joshie's mom, than any master's degreed program or job could have taught me.

So the teachers drew up a potty training plan for us and we stuck to it, and received many a punch, kick and even very deep bites from Josh as we insisted he sit on the potty, when he very simply, didn't want to. He couldn't speak at all in those days. He would just grunt, and I imagine he was VERY frustrated and possibly thought we didn't understand he didn't want to sit on the toilet, so he bit us to let us know. At the time, that was how he could communicate he didn't like something. Despite those difficult days, time goes by, and you forget how hard it was, and the practical gift of potty training is something he will always have, and oh how wonderful that is. Autonomy is a priceless gift, though it took a lot of effort.

Please also know your rights regarding your child. In order to have an IEP, or Individual Education Plan, law requires us to meet once a year with his teacher, speech pathologist, IEP coordinator, Regular Education Inclusion teacher, and sometimes his Occupational Therapist, to insure that we are all on the same page. If for some reason one of the educators or therapists just cannot be there, then don't be shy about asking for a separate meeting to further discuss your child's goals. His main teacher will prepare a list of goals that she feels are achievable, noting the frequency of times he must get them correct. It is a very specific list that covers things from basic self care, which usually is written by the Occupational Therapist, such as shoe tying, to how many times he will be able to greet a person as he enters a room. The goals change each year, as your child achieves them. And if all is going well, they will become more complex. I can remember in the beginning when they worked to teach Josh to recognize just a few letters. Now he can write them down as you say each of them, with no help whatsoever.

The first couple of years at an IEP are generally very emotional for most, as you read the goals aloud and are faced with really seeing just how little your child is able to do, or even worse, reading that they test as the age of three, when they're already six years old. However, as the years pass, and you have a comparison of how far they have come, then the IEP need not be an emotional and depressing experience. It's always easier to look back with optimism once your child has achieved such things as toilet training and speech. You just have to keep going and believing for the best outcome, and if the best is not happening, then to look at what he or she Can do, and be grateful for just that. Every gain, no matter how small, is just that, a gain, and a stepping stone to their next achievement and progression.

If one of the team members is not able to be there, you can always request a separate meeting at a later date. I reiterate this point as I have found as a former teacher, and guidance counselor, that parent involvement really does help your child get more help at school. If the people helping him know that you are very concerned, and want the best care for your son, and you are there in a positive way, respectful and such, then they will tend to take better care of your child. It's human nature, no right or wrong here. Just be involved and see. The idea of accountability doesn't hurt either. I remember as a former teacher calling parents in for a meeting. After the third call and fourth phone call and letter in two weeks, I gave up trying to contact them, and did the best I could for their son in class, knowing that there was no one he would be held accountable to at home. Parental support and involvement really does go a long way.

My other wish for Josh in the early days of his diagnosis, was that he would become super connected to people. I wanted his eye contact to return, and the affection that he used to show by cuddling and hugging to come back. His autism occurred twelve hours after the MMR (Measles, Mumps, Rubella shot). I wholeheartedly believe that he had a genetic predisposition to becoming Autistic and that the shot was just the trigger that set it off.

Ira was adopted at birth in 1965, something that has hurt his heart for almost fifty years now, not knowing his genetic roots. He really wanted to know who his biological parents were, and what his history was about, but admittedly didn't have the emotional strength to search for them. I understand his fear of searching, because I took the task on, and reading through the thousands of search ads, mom looking for son etc.. is heartbreaking business even if you are not adopted. I agreed to help Ira, and began my search in 1995 for his birth family. I spent countless hours at the New York Public Library, which looks more like a museum, searching through records of birth numbers, trying to match the only number we had on his certificate with one in a book of millions of numbers. That was entirely fruitless, but after much searching, and many phone calls to various courts and agencies, someone took pity on me, and almost ten years later, three days before I gave birth to Amalia, we had a name!

His birth mother and I connected on the telephone three days prior to my giving birth to Amalia. She is a very kind person, but very chatty just like Ira. I am rather certain, that both she and Ira could be diagnosed with Asperger's syndrome, a lighter form of Autism. They are both supremely intelligent, but hyper-focused on relaying information. Talking to Ira or his birth mom is often a very one sided conversation where-in you are the recipient of knowledge that they possess and wholeheartedly wish to impart or imprint on you. I have learned so much from Ira, but we still work on connecting more, even twenty years into our relationship.

In working towards my goal of connection for Joshua, I followed several programs whose focus was just that. Play Therapy as well as the Son Rise Program all support emotional connection. So I would just play with him making eye contact as much as possible. Now when a person pictures play with a two year old, they usually picture toys. In those dark times, Josh wouldn't look at any toys unless they were cars that he could line up. He was also fascinated with ceiling fans and trains. Occasionally a puzzle would catch his eye and we discovered that he was excellent at putting them together, once we could train his hand to follow through. Occupational Therapy and dedicated teaching and para-professional staff assisted in helping him with his fine motor skills to write and do puzzles.

So if Josh was uninterested in the cars one day, and preferred staring at the wall and poking it for 30 minutes, I would get in on the action. I would sit right next to him, and poke the wall too. If he did it once, I would say, "Mommy's going to do it once too!" in as animated a tone as I could muster. I guess my Musical Theatre training came in handy. I was every over the top character I could muster. And if I got him to look at me, I made such a big deal and praised him, and made such silly faces, that he learned from a very young age, that his responses to me Really mattered. And so it continues to this very day. However, now I'm working on toning his idea of Total control over me down... Well, sort of. It's our connection.

TEACHING

The other day we sat at the kitchen table and our very funny, and articulate daughter Amalia wrote more of her comic strip. Josh likes to imitate Amalia. He is her "Biggest Fan". In fact, if Amalia walks out of a room, Josh follows. If she closes and locks a door for some privacy, he sits outside of it, chanting her name, "Nalia, Nalia, Nalia….." It's both highly flattering to her as well as super annoying. At such times I will try and reel him back in with a promise that "She'll come back in a little bit. Let's do what Amalia was doing." Sometimes it works, sometimes it doesn't.

One time it did work, and Josh came to the kitchen table to write comics just like his heroine, super star sister. I said, "Wanna write about a cat?" Ready yourself for a stunning moment. And get used to them… Where Autism is concerned, they're Everywhere…   Josh wrote the WORD cat, "C", "A", "T" without any prompting for the first time in his life for me. Now I realize that his teachers had been working VERY hard with him, and that of course he would have made progress by now, but witnessing such a feat firsthand, is an indescribably joyful event.

I believe that our children of the spectrum have so much that they can achieve, and if given the proper opportunities, dedicated teachers, loving para-professionals, and diligent speech, occupational and physical therapists, then they will be better equipped to unleash those gifts.

After completing my master's in teaching, with a focus on the English language, I worked as a middle school teacher at a Catholic school in New York City. I loved working with my students, but discovered that teaching much of the information, such as grammar lessons, was tiresome and boring to me. Thankfully, I had free reign to create my own lessons, and thus I developed more interesting assignments for them than the teacher guides would suggest. I recall once having my twenty-five students break up into groups of five and each group was given a country to report on. One student was in charge of dress-costumes, another cuisine, history, art and other interesting facts. These types of assignments seemed to interest them most. I was still however having trouble finding ways to make lessons on pronouns more interesting, and I found that after school I was called upon more as a counselor than teacher, which I enjoyed doing. And so started my second master's degree, this time in Counseling Psychology at Fordham University.

Though I really enjoyed working with those students, I realized that teaching full time and completing my Psychology Master's was just not possible, so I finished the year and bid the school farewell. I instead became a para-professional for a young fourth grade boy with severe ADD and ADHD who attended a fancy private school in Manhattan. The work load was far less after school, with no papers to grade and parents to call, so I could attend classes and complete assignments easily. My new job simply needed me to attend school with Jack daily in order to help him to keep his focus on his work and not on disturbing other children, or simply running around and playing. In retrospect, knowing what I now know, I believe his diagnosis was probably autism, but his parents didn't say so, and the school accepted his need for a shadow or para as being due to ADD (Attention Deficit Disorder) and ADHD (Attention Deficit and Hyperactivity Disorder). I helped him for the year, and learned a lot about what para-professionals do for children in special needs classes. ALWAYS treat your para with great respect. I buy Joshie's paras gifts for every occasion, every holiday. If money is tight, make it a one dollar candy bar, but never forget them. They work hard, all day long for your child. Working with a higher functioning autistic child can be even more stressful than working with one who is severe. Josh is no longer considered severely autistic, and managing his intelligent escapades is exhausting.

Remember, a child with Autism need not resemble Rain Man... There are so many degrees of Autism, that you could be speaking with someone who is autistic and not even know it for years. Or, like myself, married to a man on the spectrum and figure it out years later. They are brilliant and occupy many a seat at local computer engineering businesses or other places of higher intelligence. In fact, I know of another child on the spectrum who is completely incapable of doing math, on paper... Yet, if you give him large numbers, he will total them in his mind within five seconds. We are privileged in our lives to live with such people. They are certainly different, and I feel and believe wholeheartedly that their gifts to us are immeasurable, though hidden at times behind the frustration they live with, due to their inability to be fully understood and to communicate like we do.

Imagine this…. You are the same person that you have always been, and then one day you awake having lost your capacity to speak. In fact, better yet, TRY it. I did. I committed myself to going one full day without talking. I didn't speak a word whatsoever for a full twenty-four hours, though I really wanted to. I became completely overwhelmed and frustrated at other people's inability to understand what I was requesting or even pointing to. I also felt left out, and at times forlorn and sad. I found myself making grunting noises, just like Joshua used to do, in order to direct people's attention to what I was trying to show them.

It was a wonderful, albeit difficult exercise in empathy and compassion. I can now say that I have a deeper understanding of the plight of the speechless autistic person. Try it yourself and you will undoubtedly be changed for the better, whether or not your autistic relative or friend is speechless.

SPEECH THERAPY

As a parent of ANY type of child, you always will question if what you are doing is correct. I recall bringing Joshua to one of the areas top speech therapy facilities in the country. We went religiously, for over sixty dollars a half hour, completely out of pocket, six times a week. Inexpensive? No. Covered by insurance? No. Helpful? Yes and definitely No.

It was helpful in that I learned to forever trust my own instinct, no matter how many degrees the person you are consulting with may have earned. There is Nothing that will serve you better than your parental intuition. Mine was screaming "No!" at me, before we even stepped foot in the facility.

I had heard that they adhered to a strict behavioral program in teaching children how to speak. Over fifteen years ago, in New York City, after I completed my second Master's degree in Counseling Psychology, I took the position of full time teacher for two years to a severely autistic child. Part of my weekly duties in addition to teaching him basic skills, self-care, reading, writing, math, was to escort him to his behavioral speech therapist once or twice a week. I didn't find it to be a pleasant or helpful intervention for the child, and at times I felt it was cruel.

I remember this New York therapist asking the boy to do a task and promising with a big fake smile that if he did, she would give him one one hundredth of a piece of cookie that she had broken up in front of him. It was a large cookie, I'll give her that. It was in fact, the very same black and white cookie that his mother bought for him daily at the corner bakery and abandoned to him entirely with a loving smile. This child ate those cookies every day and was Never made to have to work for them. I mentioned this

14

to said therapist but was brushed off and basically told to mind my own business while in her office. So I did. I sat and watched, with growing trepidation as she spoke to him, like Dolores Umbridge, the hated character from Harry Potter. I felt the tension growing, and then the sweet boy, who never once struck or bit me, in the couple of years I worked with him, laid his teeth into her and wouldn't let go. He was in Pit Bull grasp. By the way, if you are ever bit by your child, the best choice for recovery of your flesh is to Push into their mouth. Don't ever pull away as you will be pulling your flesh with their head if you push them away. Yes, this sounds counter-intuitive to what you want to do instinctively, but it works. Both Ira and I have literally saved our skin by doing so during those potty training days. So therapist, still being bit, is scolding, asking, pleading, and he isn't letting go. I ask her, "Do you want me to help?" NO she barks. Finally, about five minutes later she says, YES , Help! I said, "Sweetie, stop biting her." He let go immediately. The problem I find with some of the behavioral approach is that it's inhumane and un-empathic. She wouldn't even consider where she could meet this child. It was her way, and she was going to make him fit into it.

As I sat through session after session in speech with my own son, years later, I was reminded here and there of that time in New York. Joshie's therapist seemed to think that Josh understood what she was saying and asking him to do, but at the time, I am certain that his receptive language skills were non-existent. He maybe understood, "yes and no". Yet she was asking him to put the doll on the bed and move it to the bedroom. Really??? Joshua hated going to see her and sat session after session in complete anger, frustration and escape mode. Then one day, the last day we ever went there, his therapist said, "Michelle, we've got to break him, like a horse. It's time for you to go to the waiting room from now on."

That was the end of the "Behavioral Therapy" six month, super expensive experiment. But again, I learned several very valuable lessons.

One: Always trust your mother's or father's instinct, not the degreed people if instinct it talking

Two: If your child consistently dreads going somewhere, then stop going.

Three: I won't leave my kids alone with any professionals, except for their trusted teachers. If they don't want me in the room, there's got to be a reason. It can be a good reason, and pure, but there's the chance that it may not be good. I'm not willing to take that chance. Especially with a nonverbal child.

Four: Behavioralism doesn't work if your child has no receptive language skills…. Duh!

Five: You don't have to pay sixty-four dollars a half hour for good service. In fact, there are excellent speech therapists that charge half as much

Six: Humanism-Empathy and Love can heal better than their opposite

Seven: Trust your child in all things! Follow Their Bliss!!!

Trusting Joshua and following his bliss in the early years is what I believe made all of the difference. Everyone who meets him comments on the amazing joy that he radiates, the twinkle in his eye, the love he innately possesses and shares with all.

There are other children I see who did stay in the behavioral program that we went to, and they are often very angry children, "broken" at a young age, to follow other's whims, other's ideas, to fit into a mold that they were perhaps not meant to fit into, or ready for. They lost some of their childhood in my opinion.

Did I question my decision to pull Josh out of this esteemed program? Yes, I did. Do I regret it? Absolutely not. I am so grateful that I listened to my "mother's intuition", despite the protests of the speech people, including the developer of the program; other mother's who stuck with it and even relatives.

I'll never forget Joshua's face when I told him "Open door, we're done here. Let's go". He was so relieved when I promised him we'd never return. I still wonder why I didn't leave earlier. I guess I needed six months to figure that lesson out. Sorry Joshie…

Now, on the flip side of this coin, I want to make it clear that I do believe there IS a place for behavioral therapy, and certainly speech therapy is a must. Without behavioral intervention, Josh would be headed for status of "menace to society" and possibly wind up in jail a decade from now. However, the difference now is that he understands what we are saying, feels safe, knows that we value his feelings and preferences, and he has thus come out of his shell and is confident in this world. In fact a little too confident at times, which is why I feel it is time for some behavioral intervention, …but with heart.

.

DISCIPLINE

I have heard through the grapevine and witnessed that Thomas Trains are a favorite of many autistic children, as their faces very obviously show their emotional state, and for a sustained amount of time, which is something that is difficult for the autistic person to discern. You and I have very little problem understanding when someone is feeling sad or content, but not so for people on the spectrum, even Ira has no clue when I am upset with him, which is both a good thing and a bad. Helpful when it's just PMS upset, not so good when I feel he should know better. In the animated TV show, Thomas exaggerates each of his particular emotions, as does Percy, Henry and ALL of the other trains. Not only are they feeling sad, but sad sticks to their circular face for a LONG time. The voice over actor Sounds sad as well, sometimes in an over the top manner. Or Happy feelings aren't just a normal smile; they are an exaggerated I'm so happy I could explode kind of happy face.

Understanding that he may not understand other people's emotional states, I have endeavored to make it very clear what I am feeling when I am with Josh. There are even computer applications that will help teach this. We tried a few on the I-Pad and I was surprised at how much he didn't understand about facial expression.

Now the biggest behavioral pitfall that I have made the mistake of continually falling in, is to smile when Josh does something naughty. I may be reprimanding him at the same time and saying, "That was naughty, do not do that again." But, if there is a glimmer of a smile within, then my message is mixed, and it's already confusing enough to him, so I have to be very careful to make my message consistent and clear. Remember, no matter how amusing your child's antics are, try not to smile if they are naughty ones. Or, you will be sure to see them repeat the unwanted behavior over and over again...

One of Joshie's teacher's, Cathy Wiseman, made a home visit to discuss Joshie with me and to help set up some behavioral plans as he was completely out of control at the time. I started talking about Josh with my usual glimmer of love and excitement, and then I said, "My baby is going to be six soon." She looked at me and said, "Michelle, he's not a baby at that age."

The trap that I fell into, not an uncommon one, is to infantilize the autistic child. Josh wasn't speaking very much at the time, and he is my youngest child. Therefore, in my sensibilities, I thought of him as a little baby. More like a toddler, but you can only imagine the scenes. "Come here baby, sit on mommy's lap, let me count your toesies".... It wasn't pretty, and I am grateful that Cathy pointed it out. She was not the first, but it stuck at that point, finally.

Another thing I heard from her, that very same day, was the "Bratism vs. Autism" analogy... Now Cathy is probably one of the only people who could say that to me, as she has an adult son with Autism. She said, "Michelle, please don't take this the wrong way, but a lot of Joshie's behavior's are not due to Autism. I like to call it Bratism."

Well, She was Absolutely, unequivocally correct, and hearing it stated that way, has given me the wherewithal, to actually discipline him, GUILT FREE. His form of discipline is a time out in his room. If that doesn't stop the naughty behaviors, once he is "Let out", then I send him back and tell him he will lose his television privileges or a favored toy.

Knowing that he is acting bratty, and not just having an Autistic moment, has enabled me to stop feeling sorry for him, and to help sculpt him into a well-behaving child. Well, at least some of the time....

Here is an amusing list, (in retrospect amusing) of deviant things Josh used to do that I have put a stop to using consequences and also by controlling my laugh response;

Joshie's esteemed African American friend in his classroom has corn rolls in his hair and Josh apparently decided that if he could get me out of the room, then he would endeavor to give himself a "new do" like his buddy. He asked me to leave him alone by saying, "Pivacy" for "Privacy". I agreed and left him, but after ten minutes of silence I started to get a little nervous, so I yelled down the stairs, "You okay down there buddy?" He screamed back, "GO AWAY!" That's when I knew there was a problem, so I walked down the stairs only to find such a scene that I fell to my knees in horror and shock while simultaneously laughing and crying, something I had never achieved before that moment... He had taken his kid scissors to his head and cut forty circles into his hair in an effort to replicate his friends do. He was so proud that I didn't actually employ a consequence. I was kinda of proud of him as well, just for having taken the initiative, and of course, for sweeping it up.

Natural Consequence: Just having to trim it up for him later was natural consequence enough, as he really hates having his hair cut and thus has only had to suffer them twice a year and most of the time from me in his sleep, due to his absolute terror of the haircut.

If Josh was angry enough at Ira or I, for being sent to time out, he would stop in his tracks, on the way to the time out and urinate on the floor.

Consequence: He had to clean it up with a towel

One day Josh decided to go into the pantry. He was in there for about 4 minutes. Now it is a large pantry and I had Lite Brite in there for him to play with in the daytime, so I went to check in on him and he said, "Go Away!" Again always a bad sign... I of course ran to the pantry, opened the pantry door and to my utter shock and disbelief, Josh had an artistically sensorally inspired moment, that didn't involve Lite Brite. He found the Halloween Orange flavored Oreo's and painted the entire pantry with them.

Consequence: What I did and what I should have done are two different stories. I should have had him clean it, but he had also painted himself in Oreo orange filling, so he went directly into the shower. He was Very displeased, as he was still attached to finishing his art in the pantry, and so being swiftly moved to the shower was a pretty bad "natural" consequence for him. I then personally cleaned the pantry, as the thought of him cleaning that, was too terrifying. And it turns out, that Oreo cookie filling is VERY oily and difficult to remove. What I should have done was to have him also clean the mess he made in the pantry, but my own interest in cleanliness won out.

Josh is fascinated with door handles. I have locks on all the bedroom doors so that he cannot go in and just take whatever he wishes, which was at one time a common pastime for him. Unfortunately after we installed the locks, Josh saw me hide the nail that we use to unlock each door, up high on top of a picture frame. When I had walked away, he devised a scheme to get my nail down by throwing stuffed animals at it. He was successful and I later found a myriad of nails in a stash in his room. The child is very resourceful. I never let his autism label, innocent looks and former inability to speak, fool me. A lot is going on in his mind, and it's very intelligent.

Consequence: He had to personally apologize and give me back the nails. I also made him sit in a time out for sneaking into my room and for stashing the nails away.

One of my favorite stories of deviant behaviors is a fairly recent one which occurred at school when he left his Autism Classroom that he spends most of the day in with five other children on the spectrum. For an hour of each day he goes to a regular education class with approximately twenty-five "typically" functioning children. This is called, "Inclusion" for him. He has a para-professional accompany him, sometimes they are called, "Shadows" just as I had been in NYC for the boy with severe ADHD. The job of the shadow, is to do just that. Shadow the child, stay in the background, but be there to help keep the child on track, as much as is required, moment to moment. This is not a job for someone who cares to daydream. Your total focus   is   on   high   alert.

So the other day while in his inclusion classroom, Josh became tired of the bright fluorescent lights, went to the light switch and turned them off. Many autistic children have sensory sensitivity to light, especially the flourescent light used in schools. Josh has a love hate relationship with the lights in our home as well. Nevertheless, he was directly instructed not to do that again, and he complied. Sounds good so far. However, he probably didn't like that verdict, so he decided to rebel in a different way and he expressed his dissatisfaction by taking another child's work from them. He was of course stopped, but since he knew better he was given a consequence.

At the end of his hour of inclusion, he was told that he lost his "Gummy Worm" reward that Miss Cathy gives him each day during their lessons and after inclusion. Josh is accustomed to being given a reward for good behavior after inclusion, so this certainly distressed him. Children on the spectrum tend to enjoy the predictability of routine, so he was very upset at this change of circumstance. In fact, it distressed him enough that he actually grabbed the gummy worm and stuffed it into his mouth. His para at the time told him, "No Josh, you didn't behave well today, so you can't have that now. Give it back." He eventually gave it back to her, from his mouth. She threw it away in front of him.

I have received many notes this past week about his naughty behavior, and so will you, so take it in stride. It seems that this happens in waves. There will be several months that Josh is behaving perfectly well, and then out of nowhere, he starts acting up again. So I confronted him with the latest report from his speech therapist, which stated that he was "Really throwing his weight around today, as well as toys in her room." I told Josh that I read his report, and I detailed all of the naughty things it said he did, and I assured him that I would be reading it every day, and if there were anymore naughty reports, that he would lose his television hour in his room at night. He said his usual "No" as his verbal way of protesting this decision. I assured him I would do just that, and that he had better behave. He ran into my arms and kissed my cheek and said, "I love you mommy". Don't misunderstand this. He didn't do that for love. He did that because he knows how much I love his sweet "I Love you's". And yes, I smiled, but I assured him that I still meant what I said. He walked away...

So the next day, he came into the house and while I was preparing snacks, he took his communication notebook out of his backpack and hid it in his bedroom. The communication notebook is the notebook in which his teacher Miss Cathy and his paraprofessional helper of the day write about what occurred at school. I read it daily and will write in it as well to give them information on what he did over the week-end, or even to warn them of a loose tooth. I guess that he figured if he hid it then I wouldn't be able to read it, and he'd be off the hook completely. I must admit that I was rather proud internally of this approach, as it showed initiative and cunning. He had made an intelligent attempt, unsavory though it may be in nature to remedy a problem. Nevertheless, when I threatened with the loss of tomorrow mornings tablespoon of coffee in his rice milk, he acquiesced and returned the notebook. He's a clever one all right.

And don't judge... The only way he'll drink rice milk and get any calcium into his body, as it is calcium fortified, is if there's a teaspoon of mommy's coffee in it...

Please note that each naughty antic mentioned above is either followed by a "Natural Consequence" or a Consequence of my choosing. If in your pity for your child, you choose to ignore problem behaviors, trust me, they will only grow and so will your little tyke. It is far easier to stop the problematic behaviors when they are small, versus when they are a towering teenager. If a natural consequence does not occur, then impose one, and do so consistently. It is a loving gesture to use a Stop sign, and an irresponsible parenting move to just let them wander about aimlessly.

Since Josh is so attached to predictable routines, I oftentimes will simply take away a favored routine. Each day when Josh gets off of his bus, he runs up the driveway, gets undressed in the laundry, room, runs to his room to get into one of his long comfy t-shirts, formerly mine. He then washes his hands with my coaxing, and sits down to a healthy snack.

I often give him seaweed chips, bananas, fresh water smoked salmon, not the farm raised, or even a doughnut, in order to fatten him up a little. After that he expects cuddle time on the recliner and then he likes to play Nintendo, followed up by him taking out all of the vintage fisher price houses that I have collected and lining them up. I have hundreds of little people that he can play with in a red bin and that comes out as well. He can play like that for an hour sometimes. Amalia comes home shortly after and they play Badminton in the house, and eventually we have dinner, then watch Spongebob Squarepants for an hour. This routine is what occurs almost every day, with minor tweaks. It must comfort him, because he doesn't really stray much from these activities. Sometimes I'll have a gardening, bike riding or baking idea, but generally we stick to the above list, especially in the winter. If he were to lose his Spongebob time he would be very upset. It is rare nowadays that I have to take anything away, but just having the threat there helps to keep him on track, and to stop engaging in bad behaviors as well.

SENSES

Offering Josh (and typical functioning kids for that matter), different activities is Very important, and will stave off their exploration into alternative unseemly avenues, such as stealing nails or painting pantries. Satisfying your child's sensory system is of utmost importance. Here are some ways to do just that.

Some of Josh's favorite fun activities have involved great creativity. If you're not already offering these to your child, then consider the following: The old time Shrinky dinks are fun to color and then you have the added bonus of getting to watch them shrink! Play-doh (especially for its sensory benefits of having to touch and mold the Play-doh) has always been a favorite in our home, and Josh will make all sorts of figures out of them.

I recall years ago, when Josh was too sensitive to touch things such as Play-doh, we were directed to purchase a large box and to fill it with rice, and to hide favorite little play things inside of it for him to find. At the time of this sensory box, he was really into dinosaurs, so to Costco I went and bought forty pounds of rice. Then to the dollar store for tiny dinosaurs. At first Josh wouldn't dare touch the rice to find the dinosaurs hidden beneath. It was explained to me by an Occupational Therapist, that sometimes things hurt him, or make his body feel bad to the touch, such as rice. Other times, an Autistic person might touch a light bulb for a long time and feel nothing, burning their fingers nonetheless. I also learned that it goes back and forth and so I'd always watch to see if he was having an overly sensitive day, or an under sensitive day.

Having the rice vat was helpful in "Desensitizing" Josh to the strange feelings his body felt when touching the rice. I recall him screaming and not wanting to touch it, for the first few times I opened the box, even despite the toys he could see peeking out. He even was smart enough to get a tool to move the rice around and get to the toys touch free. This was somewhat heartbreaking to observe, but over time, Josh just dug his hand down into the vat of rice and ultimately years later has become desensitized enough to play outside in our sand box, burying his feet entirely! In fact, playing in the sand is one of his favorite summer things to do nowadays. I wonder if he would be so inclined and interested, had we not had the rice box the occupational therapist recommended...?

On the other hand, rainy days around here have been a nuisance for poor Josh, as one thing that he has not entirely outgrown, is his dislike of water on his body, when not of the predictable nature, such as washing hands or bathing. He most of the time enjoys being in the pool, bathtub or shower, and making bubbles, but if a drop of water gets onto his clothing, FORGET About it...

I believe it just feels, "wrong" to him. I can completely relate to that, but on a much smaller scale. When I walk into the kitchen and get water on my socks, it usually bothers me and I feel the need to change them. However, walking Josh to the bus, and getting water on my pants or jacket, doesn't faze me. It really bothers the little guy however. On any given "rain" day, you can see Josh taking his slow stroll to the bus, turtle speed, because his hands are holding his pants up to his knees, so that the bottom edge does not get wet.

Sensory issues need not involve the sense of touch alone. Josh still covers his ears as a siren looms outside, in a loud mall, or any area with a lot of conversation going on. Ira has explained to me that he can personally hear all conversations simultaneously and so perhaps that is why Josh will seem overwhelmed in those situations. He seems to become either agitated or withdrawn. It's as if he responds by going into an invisible shell and withdrawing, or he seemingly attempts to combat the sounds, by making even louder noises himself. Either way, not so good. We still avoid malls and large crowded events where there will be a lot of people. He has become more adept at going into malls over time, but we have come to the conclusion, that desensitization is great for things that one Must do. On the other hand, not everyone must go to a baseball game, so after two summers of failed attempts to keep him interested in playing on the local Miracle League team, we have acquiesced and happily follow his lead to more natural environments with less people, such as a park with no baseball game going on...

Josh is also fascinated with his sense of sight. He used to love staring at ceiling fans. In fact, one of his first play dates, with a classmate also on the spectrum, involved the boy coming over, running from room to room, and turning every light switch on that he could find. That would have been no problem with me, but at that time, Josh had an aversion to lights, and so he followed his buddy around turning them off...Not your typical conflict, but certainly, not your typical kids. The rest of their play date was centered on the ceiling fans in each room. They ran from room to room turning them on, lying underneath them, and laughing as if they both understood a really funny joke that no one else was privy to. I think that the next time he has a play date I will pull out the Lite Brite as well...

I had never been so aware of my senses before having Joshua. He is fascinated by ALL sorts of smells, and for a long time there, I had trouble with him tugging at my arm, pulling it up, and stuffing his little nose in my arm-pit. Yes, in my arm-pit. Especially after a sweaty workout. He was obsessed. I guess he loves his mommy....LOL... Obviously this type of a behavior is well, just gross, so I did eventually put a stop to it, and he settled for holding and smelling my worn t-shirts instead. He now wears them and sleeps in them as his pajamas.

Joshua also used to be obsessed with girls clothing and preferred high heels and pink colored dresses from his sister's wardrobe to anything as dull as "boy clothes", so my oversized t-shirts are actually an improvement. Don't get me wrong here. I indulged. Did I ever. To the scowls of caring family members and friends who thought I was going to make him gay, or a sissy so they would tell me. First of all, to them I say, Thank you for your concerns, but at the age of two and three and even four years old, I wasn't very worried. He just liked acting like his older sister. If he had an older brother I am certain he would have been trying to raid "his" closet instead. However, I will say that when Joshua turned almost six years old, and started trying to wear the dresses to school, I changed my mind. So, nowadays, he gets my worn t-shirts, in blue, green, and an occasional red.

Please remember to remind others to be sensitive to your sensory sensitive child. I have no qualms about asking people to use quieter voices around Josh when I can sense he is approaching overload. Nowadays he will actually speak up for himself and say, "Too Loud", but if you see your sweetie covering their ears and grimacing as if in pain, then why not leave the environment, or ask people to settle their voices down. I can't imagine anyone with any heart complaining. Remind them if they do, that your child hears their voice times one hundred its volume. Whether it is true or not, it registers in people's brains and they will quiet down when you explain it like that, nine out of ten times.

FOODS

When we first moved to Michigan Ira's greatest complaint was the lack of good restaurants here. Having grown up in Riverdale New York, Ira's parents would take him for Dim Sum to China Town every Sunday morning. It was a great time for him and the wait staff adored him there, as he would pick up his soup bowl and drink the soup out of it, no qualms. He still does that today, despite my embarrassment at it. They also respected his dad HD, who can be best described to look like Mr. Crabs from the Krusty Crab on Spongebob Squarepants. Seriously. They wear the exact same outfit, and more. When HD goes to China Town they hand him the bill each time with taxes included, but he knows that if you're Chinese, then they won't charge you taxes, so HD who is Jewish with curly gray hair and not one Asian feature immediately hands them back the bill and says, "I'm Chinese". They take the taxes off every time, for fifty years now... Dining out with Ira and his Dad is a "special" experience, but not always. Ira has many food allergies and often times his throat will swell to dangerous widths. In fact, he recently had his esophagus stretched so as to avoid choking to death. Ira is not the only one with food allergies that I know.

I would be remiss if I just skipped over a discussion on food allergies and autism... Most kids on the spectrum have them, and in abundance. There are kids who are allergic to so many things, that all they can eat is rice, certain vegetables and hot dogs or deli meat. We had Joshua's blood tested and no shock there, he too was allergic to the typical culprits, All dairy, peanuts, and soy, as well as peas and garlic. Your doctor can have a blood test performed to find out what he is allergic to. It was nice to know the results, but even prior to receiving the results I had taken him completely off of soy, dairy, wheat gluten and anything with corn in it. And aspartame or any other fake sugar is akin to poison in my book. There are studies proving its hazards and fake sugars, as well as MSG are all additives that I will not ingest, nor will I allow my kids to touch. Anything that says "Diet" or Sugar free is truly dangerous. Look it up for yourselves. It always pains me to overhear a parent ordering their kid a "diet coke". If they have diabetes, then just have them drink water with lemon in it, or buy flavored seltzer drinks. I enjoy Peach-Pear La Croix water, nothing artificial about it. Get creative! Try dropping fruit into water and let it infuse the water. People are ignorantly, slowly killing themselves with fake sugars that should never have been allowed on the market in the first place.

Food really can change people's moods. Joshie's behavior becomes very aggressive after eating soy and corn. Unfortunately, after weaning him off of my breast milk, his next milk was pure soy... I certainly beat myself up for that one, for way too long, but all we can do about past mistakes is learn from them and move on... And so we did. For a year or so, Josh ate a lot of Quinoa pasta, gluten free pasta, rice, broccoli, bananas, hot dogs, and 100 percent berry juice, juice boxes.

Never did we stray from that formula, even during the surprise drop by's from well meaning relatives with pizza's in hand. The child who is allergic tends to crave the foods that irritate him the most, and pizza was always a big one for Josh. We helped him through many a meltdown when those foods were being denied, and we would even risk souring our relationships with family and friends and asking them to take their pizzas to the car. We kept him "clean" for one year.

I wish I could say definitively what that accomplished. What I am able to accurately report, is that Josh did become more engaged that particular year. He made more eye contact and he seemed less frustrated than in the past. He also learned how to communicate the answer "Yes" and "No" by shaking his head appropriately. Until that point, we couldn't get a straight answer from him. He couldn't tell us what was wrong, and he couldn't even answer a question such as, "Are you hungry?" It was very sad, frustrating for all, and difficult. When Josh learned to nod correctly, a whole new world of communication, autonomy and personal power opened to him, much to our relief.

He made it very clear with his "NO" nod, that he was not interested in eating broccoli, but "YES" he wanted another hot dog. We felt like lotto winners. Our boy was opening up. He had opinions, not just screams and grunts of frustration.

I am glad that we did the diet in retrospect. I recall going to health food stores to find wheat free, gluten free, soy free and dairy free products. Yes, those foods tasted like I imagine cardboard tastes, but at least they were "safe" foods for him.

There was even a site that made it easy for newcomers to try new foods. I ordered a large sample box with a variety of products to see what he would eat or reject. There weren't very many winners, but once you find even one new product in such a limited diet, you're really rolling. I am also happy to report to you, that all of those foods are now significantly less expensive than they were five years ago. With so many health conscious folk, as well as celiac disease sufferers, and autism on the rise (1 in 68), the prices in this category have actually gone down. I used to pay up to seven dollars for a box of gluten free pasta which can now be found for a quarter of that price.

Fast forward a few years, and Joshua is now eating pizza once a week at school in the lunchroom with his other friends in his class of six students. I don't serve him pizza more often than once a week, but I feel that now that he has come so far, has normal stools, and is talking well, that it is okay to experiment a little. It took us several years to get to this pizza eating point, as many experiments yielded crazy behaviors and sore stomachs, but now that his system is more mature, he tolerates it all right.

I am still afraid of soy products, corn, and milk. His oatmeal has "Rice" milk poured over it, or "almond milk" instead. I wholeheartedly believe that soy milk is like poison to his system. Ira believes that corn or corn syrup makes him act like a loon, and since Ira actually does statistical data in his head by heart, I believe he is right.

In retrospect, Josh is far luckier than some of his comrades at school. There are children so allergic to nuts and milk, that even smelling them can set them off into serious health issue territory which can even end their lives. They have to eat in "Safe rooms" and I can only imagine how nervous their parents are sending them to school each day. EpiPens sit ready in the teacher's drawer.

It is my very highest recommendation that if you have a child on the spectrum, or have any influence with someone who does, that you have a blood allergy test done. They can do the other kind of allergy test, which is best described as scrapes on the back, but that can be very painful to a person without sensory issues let alone one with them. At least the blood test just consists of one poke, and not a long torturous process like I have heard the other test described to be. I recommend the allergy test, because there are foods that can really make it harder for the children to function. No, I am not a doctor, not even a nurse, but I have seen what the removal of certain foods has done for our son, and there is a reason so many thousands of kids are put on similar diets. It just might work for yours as well.

I am absolutely of the "leave no stone unturned" mentality. When I first was able to start reading books on autism again, without sobbing so hard that I couldn't see, one of the first ones I tackled was Jenny McCarthy's book "Louder than Words" about her son Evan and their journey. I decided then, after crying through virtually Every single page, that I would do exactly what Jenny did for her son, since he is so much better. This is why I suggest trying the diet, not for a week or two, but for at least a month and definitely take notes. See if you find any improvements occurring. If the thought of taking notes puts you into super stress mode, then just do the diet. I say this, because I remember how stressful it was at that time, and I didn't always adhere to my note taking goal, but the few that I did take were really helpful later.

Now that we've discussed food, let's talk poop. After Josh became Autistic, his autism stemmed from the Measles, Mumps, Rubella shot trigger, we noticed he was having loose bowel movements, about six times a day. What was formerly a normal bowel movement, was now diarrhea, and perpetually so.

We had his stools tested. The doctor ordered a home kit for us, and for three days, I dug into his stool samples and put small amounts into various containers as instructed. The results were astounding. His report stated that he had NO normal bacterial flora in his stomach. Josh was experiencing "leaky gut", something that a lot of autistic kids endure. The only medicinal supplement that Josh has consistently taken has been Klaire Labs, Pro-Thera Vital 10 powder, which is a pro-biotic of the highest concentration. We sprinkle it on his food every morning, for the past 5 years now as it has no taste. There have been a couple of occasions that we decided to test and see if he could go without it, and unfortunately the diarrhea re-occurred.

Again, not a doctor, or nurse, but if all of his food was just going straight through, then how much of it was actually getting to his brain I have wondered. We order it on ice once a month, and are excessively grateful for this product. Please do note, that the pro-biotic that is not refrigerated, will not work. Thus the order is shipped on ice. Don't waste your time with un-refrigerated store bought pro-biotics, as they are usually far too weak to make any impact whatsoever. Our Pro-Thera Vital 10 powder costs us 40.40 each time shipping included and is well worth every penny.

When I was in the "No stone unturned" phase, I even administered Vitamin B shots myself, as our doctor at the time suggested giving them to him. He also had the best tasting cod liver oil we could find. It was lemon infused and truly had no fishy taste to it. While I don't believe these things harmed him at all, I am also uncertain as to whether they helped or not.

There was one vitamin-supplement-chemical that the doctor, more scientist than doctor, wanted to try out on him. Mother's intuition said no, but we were seeing no improvements and so I figured let's try it. He seemed to regress rapidly on that, and so I stopped it after four days.

On this journey, you will be faced with so many options, so many modalities to choose from, so please remember to trust that small voice within. If it doesn't feel right, then it probably is wrong.

Most amazingly, I had been praying quite diligently for help in checking off every modality that I had decided to use for Joshua's recovery, and one of our weekly teenage volunteers from the Friendship Circle for special needs children, came by with her father one Sunday. Her dad is a doctor, and stood in our hallway with a kind smile. He humbly offered his hyperbaric oxygen chamber for our use on Josh if we'd like, no charge, totally a gift out of the kindness of his heart. I started sobbing, as I was so touched by his extraordinary generosity, but also because it was truly the only thing left on my mental list that we had not done for our boy.

In the end we declined his generosity, and I emphasize the word generosity. Hyperbaric oxygen treatments can run above five thousand dollars a month. Since Josh was doing so well at that time, we didn't feel that it was worth the risk, and in prayer God instructed me to decline. Nevertheless, you do meet some very good and generous people on your autism road...

Prayer has become a huge part of my life nowadays. The determination that I formerly had relied on has faded and I am very grateful for divine intervention and request it daily.

Also, make sure to ask your Occupational Therapist about something called "Brushing". Josh is "brushed" at school each morning with a therapeutic brush on his legs and arms and at home over summer vacation as well. This simple five minute intervention is very useful in helping their system to regulate well. Don't just start brushing on your own however. There is a specific way and a specific brush to use. Your OT can show you proper brushing technique.

We also found different musical modalities helpful. Ask your Occupational Therapist about CD's created for the autistic person. Some are supposed to help to calm them, others will help activate the speech centers. We lived off of the one titled "Peach Jamz" for a long time and it did help to calm him significantly. Always have the headset cord hanging off of the left ear, not the right.

To Do

1. Have an allergy blood test done
2. Try the Wheat Free, Dairy Free, Soy Free, Gluten Free diet for at least a month and note changes (Do diet no matter what blood test yields)
3. Never give your kids Aspartame, Sucralose or other artificial sweeteners. Also, order your Chinese food with NO MSG or Corn Starch (the cleaner the food the better)
4. Try a higher protein diet with rice, fresh fruit and vegetables
5. If your child has stomach issues, talk to your doctor about getting a highly concentrated Pro-biotic Pro-Thera Vital 10
Klaire labs sends it on ice (1-888-488-2488)
6. Pray, A lot..
7. Talk to your OT about starting "Brushing"
8. Talk to your OT about Music therapy and special CD's such as Peach Jamz

9. Feed your child brocolli daily

EATING OUT

Dining out is typically thought of as a pleasure, a treat, an experience to look forward to, where one does not have to think about what groceries to buy, what foods to prepare in advance and ultimately to cook later. Not so much for our family... Cooking for an hour and a half is far more pleasurable than having the four of us dine out together. Well, at least most of the time. Certainly in the beginning....

In his early autism days, Josh would stand on the booth or chair, and we would tell him to sit down. He would comply, but then a few moments later, up he'd shoot, and between having to keep him "grounded" and being aware of the older women shaking their head's at us as if we were awful parents, it just felt overwhelming. I remember crying at many a dinner out, as the other stares from people who had empathy and understood he was, well, "special', only made my hurting heart overflow with tears. It was as if all I needed was a sympathetic nod from an understanding stranger, to unleash all the sorrow I had bottled up inside. And then they'd pour forth uncontrollably.

I kept it together most everywhere else, but somehow, restaurants were a trigger. What really caused the hurt and sorrow was that I could see how they saw Joshua, not how I saw Joshua. I saw every small improvement and grasped onto it as if he had just won a Nobel peace prize. What I saw as an improvement, in their eyes was still just, not right, sad, backwards, not good enough. They didn't say any of this to me, no. I just intuited from their "I'm so sorry for that kid and family" stares, that they thought he was really behind. That look typically burst my bubble of lies that I told myself, about how great he was doing, when he really wasn't doing that well. On the other hand, I find it excessively important to praise the good improvements that your child makes, and if the only thing that he is doing better, is "NOT hitting" his head on the wall any longer, or rubbing his feces into it, then hey, stick with it until you have something else to add to your internal list.

I remember a funny restaurant outing. Josh was terrified of flying bugs at the time and would scream louder than a siren if he saw one. Yeah, you know where this is going.

Winter is a fantastic time for us. It's a break from the flying bug phobia. But of course, this day was a gorgeous summer day and I thought that it might be nice to go to the local Greek diner for some family bonding and eating out time. We sat at a window. BAD idea… That's where all of the flies go. They want out of the diner and windows attract them. Please take note of that if you have a bug phobe child as well.… Lo and behold a fly, nay, two flies flew to our window. Joshua screamed such a Loud, blood curdling scream, that absolutely every single one of the sixty people in the restaurant stopped talking, turned our way, and stared. All except my friend Jen, the mother of his also autistic little friend who happened to be at the same restaurant. She was still talking to her mother at another booth, completely oblivious to the scream. I guess her sweetie has desensitized her to blood curdling screams as well… So I picked him up and took him outside. Unfortunately, there were more flies out there and people eating at the tables outside were now also involved. We left.

So dining out still occurs, but not as often, or, we go at odd hours such as five pm for dinner, or two pm for a late lunch, when the restaurants are far less crowded, just in case. We've learned that we can do what other typically functioning families do, but just at different times.

Another time we were at the same Greek restaurant, he decided that he had to sit on the stools at the bar and started to kick and yell to get his way. All I needed was thirty seconds to make him understand that "No meant No", but a nasty woman said, "Can't you discipline your child? Geez". Now I understand completely, that if you're dining out that you want some peace and quiet. True. I don't think that hearing a kid push his weight around with his parents should be part of your package deal, but she didn't even give us thirty seconds, and she was rude. And, PS, Lady.… Try going to a more adult type restaurant next time if you hate hearing kids.

I have always flirted with the idea of purchasing business cards that say, "My son has Autism, sorry if there's a little noise at times, but we thought it better to take him out into society, rather than lock him in the house for the rest of his life…"……………………

I have heard of one local mother who wears a t-shirt that says something to the affect of, "Ask me anything about Autism". Case CLOSED!!! I am betting that no one will bother that woman...

Unfortunately, there are still people, and some loud mouthed clueless celebrities, who want to say that Autism doesn't exist, that it's just "Bad parenting". Thanks for the support there. I'm being sarcastic of course. Why don't you go to the Sudan next and tell them that there haven't been millions of people murdered and tortured there too. Or, call up a Holocaust survivor and tell them they made it up. Please. Don't get me started. Let's leave it at that....

SAFE PLACES

There are however, some places that are "Safe Places" where no one will bother you or give you nasty looks or throw disparaging comments your way, or even send that empathic gaze that makes you cry. We go to a wonderful place called, "The Friendship Circle". This is solely Ira's job, and I know that when he is there, that the kids are in an environment that is supportive. It offers membership to people with kids who have "Special Needs". Members can come to their facility to play in one of their many rooms, ranging from two full gyms, a room with swings and ball pit, a play kitchen, a water room, art room, sensory room with groovy lights and sounds, and an entire village with real traffic lights and bikes. There is also a library, pet store with a wide range of animals to care for, movie theatre, bank and full service salon. They offer classes on social skill development, as well as practical classes on how to ride a bike. Everyone there is in the same boat, living with one disorder or another, and so the "Bad parenting" looks are out the door. Pressure is off.

FC as we call it for short, also offers a variety of classes and camps and they even send volunteer teens to your home to play with your kid once a week! My daughter is in a class called, "Sibs Night". It is open to children who have a special needs sibling. Nothing like bonding with people who really "Get you". She loves it.

Definitely check on-line if there is a Friendship Circle near you, or similar program.

When Joshua didn't understand what we were saying, we would sing, hoping that sounds and tunes would stick and bring familiar recall. Our song for Friendship circle was, "Friendship circle, friendship circle, friendship circle, going to the friendship cir-ir-cle". Eventually if Josh wanted to go there he would just hum the tune without the words, but we understood and obliged.

They have also catered to the parents and have get-together's for mom's only, or Dad's only, such as a spa night for the moms, or an outing to a game for the dads. They offer group therapy for the parents, and though I have been unable to attend due to scheduling issues, I really would have liked to sit with other mom's and dads' and vent a bit, as well as to hear stories that I can relate to about their spectrum children.

I personally started a small group outing a few years back. It lasted for about a year. Once a month we mom's of spectrum children would meet at a nice restaurant for dinner, a glass of wine, and good conversation. At first, we had said that this would be reserved as a "no autism discussion" time. Again, how funny that is… Let's just put it this way, you get three or four spectrum mom's together, and stories will definitely fly. And it was good. It was cathartic to hear about how little Johnny started to talk, or how another child was finally potty trained. We'd celebrate our small successes and also share tips with one another. I listened and took mental notes and applied what I felt would help. I'm certain they did as well. It was also useful to discuss delinquency problems and hear helpful tips on how to deal with peeing on the floor behaviors for example. I'm fairly certain someone in that dinner group told me to make him clean it up himself. They were right. Whoever they were.

SIBLINGS

For any of you who have other children who are typically functioning, I highly urge you to make special time to take them out to dinner or lunch and to really give them your full attention. As much as I adore my daughter, and as much as she deserves my undivided attention, Joshua is tough competition. She may be in the middle of speaking to me, and he will literally come straight to me, plop on my lap, and turn my head with his two hands towards his face, not letting go, and thus stealing Amalia of my focus. Now, you may think, "Well, get him off of your lap, and make him let go of your face". Sure, that happens often. Still, he will continue off of my lap to vie for my attention, and eventually Amalia will just say forget it, let's talk later. Sometimes later doesn't come because other things come up.

Because of my awareness of her loss of attention, I have implemented a Mandatory Girl's week-end at a local Hotel or Bed and Breakfast, once, every three months. Yes the getaway locale is only a city or two over, and only twenty minutes from our home, but that doesn't stop us. It feels like a glorious vacation, something to look forward to, a respite where "everybody knows your name". And, yes, they're always glad we came. After doing this for the past five years, the hotel wait staff know us, we know them, and they are very supportive of Amalia and treat her as a princess when she is there.

We were there one Christmas break, and three of the wonderful waitresses were up to something, we could tell. They all approached our table, smiles bubbling over, holding a velvet platter with various jeweled barrettes on it. We had seen them selling those barrettes earlier, for anything between twenty-five and fifty dollars. They were so generous to us, and with heartfelt tears in their eyes, they said, "Amalia, we would be honored if you would take one of these. You are such a good person and sister and we want you to pick anyone that you would like." Amalia picked the smallest one, a quartz crystal hair clip and we were so touched. That kindness and memory will never fade.

We are going back in ten days from now. The countdown is on. We Love it there and are very blessed to be able to do this every couple of months or so. Most importantly, she feels extra special, with no distractions from her brother. And I always leave the Hotel experience thinking, "Wow! How wonderful to bond with her like this. I didn't realize that she has grown so much." I always walk away thinking that it is unfair to her that she doesn't always get this type of attention. Inevitably, for the next month after our getaway, I plan special after school trips with her to local restaurants and coffee shops and we play UNO and bond some more. Perhaps after this next trip I will extend those special times until our next Hotel outing, not allowing the world of Josh and Autism to distract me from my other sweet angel.

What can you do to make your other children feel special? If you're a grand-parent, call your son or daughter up and offer to take care of the other child for a day. You have no idea how far that goes in helping the entire family. I'm certainly excessively grateful when my mom does that, and both she and Amalia always have a great time.

If finances are a current concern, then just taking your sibling child out to a park, local diner, for a walk around the block, or to a coffee shop with UNO cards will serve just as well. Lack of money is no excuse. Take them out for some Autism-free time, you'll never regret it, and they will benefit so enormously for having been made to feel extra special.

As the caregiver of a person on the spectrum we know how difficult things can get. But just imagine being a young child and having to deal with the situations that arise. Growing up is hard enough, but add a sibling on the spectrum to the mix and you will find some of the most stressed out, but totally amazing kids on the planet. Our Amalia fits the bill. She has had to grow up far faster than the average child her age, due to her brother's, let's say, Idiosyncracies...

Children with special needs siblings learn to be more patient, compassionate and self-less because of their siblings special needs. That is why I often take Amalia out alone or make sure that Josh is out so that she can enjoy some uninterrupted house time where she can even bring things out that her brother would otherwise become obsessed with and try and take over. I realize that the same things can happen with two or more typically functioning siblings, but the difference is that sometimes, especially in the younger years, the autistic sibling truly doesn't understand that what they are doing is wrong, and so it places the parents in a position to hope, pray and sometimes plead with the typically functioning sibling to "just let him play with it." Not fair, not even right at times, but sometimes it happens. When faced with what you know will be a forty-five minute scream-fest wherein your child will attempt over and again to beat his head on the wall, or the option of the sibling just relinquishing the toy that they were playing with, and picking out a new one, then the relinquishing of the toy seems a better choice, especially after you just started your PMS and got in a fight with your husband. I can't even begin to count the number of toys that Amalia has kindly given to Josh to play with, and then I have gone out and bought a duplicate for her, just for the sake of peace. Don't judge. I know I'm not the only one…

In the positive, our daughter is best described as a solid and grounding force in the midst of chaos, in any circumstance. She is truly wise beyond her years and has a sense of humor that is amazing. She is sweet and kind and sensitive and empathic to others. She cares about people and animals and has a superior intellect. In fact she was tested and her IQ is supremely high, probably in part due to Ira and his intellectual downloads. As his daughter, she hangs on every word he has to say. I have by now tuned out the downloads, but she listens, and the information she has is extravagant for a nine year old. I have letters from every single teacher she has had through the years which state how impressed they are with her, and how kind and sweet she is. We are very blessed indeed.

I was recently at a function where I was seated next to a woman who happened to be a special needs teacher and the sibling of a special needs brother. I spoke of Amalia and how I worried that she was sometimes getting the short end of the stick and her response to me was one that I had never heard before and it certainly made me feel better especially coming from her. She said that she grew up like Amalia did, and realized that her parents were doing the best that they could for both of them, but that her brother often required more attention. She claimed that it made her far more empathic and interested in helping others which makes her feel good to this day, as she is a special needs teacher and has been one for about thirty years. I was so pleased to hear that she understood and that it has been a positive aspect of her life, not something she feels badly about for having experienced. She in no way felt as if she got the short end of the stick.

I believe it is very important to show gratitude to your sibling child, to let them know you completely understand their frustrations with their autistic sibling, and that it is okay for them to feel what they feel, as their sibling can truly be very frustrating. I also have the added bonus of describing to Amalia that I was the oldest of four children, and that all three of my siblings presented different challenges to me, but that I was enriched from having grown up with them. She then asked if we were going to have another child. I told her "No", which comforted her immediately...

Some of the more trying times of being Josh's sibling would occur when he would often say her name over and over and over again. He would call her name for hours, anytime she would walk away from him. Fortunately he doesn't do that any longer. But had I not shown Amalia empathy for her annoyance from him, then she could have felt very alone, isolated and wrong about having her feelings in the first place, which is unhealthy. I helped her to vent her feelings, and continue to do so. There were years when you would not see the four of us together in the house until dinner time, because Josh was so obsessed with following her around and imitating her back then that we would just stay out of the house with her. Being followed around like that puts a lot of pressure on anyone, and even more so on a child.

Some of my best times through these past ten years have absolutely been spent with Amalia on girl vacations at a hotel or bed and breakfast. Again, if you are financially unable to do that, then ask a friend to allow you to stay at their house for a night or two to take a break. People can't know how much of a prisoner you can be in your very own home, when your special needs child won't allow you to do anything but cater to him. And if you decide to play a game or watch a show, how miserable they can make it for the whole family if they don't want you to do that, by self-harming when pre-verbal, or even defecating all over the house in protest, or stealing and destroying things. As I write this, it sounds as if we lived in a war zone, and truly we felt like prisoners during those tough years. Time outs are a wonderful thing, but total peace is not possible even if your child does acquiesce and go on a time out. The screaming or banging is nerve racking and when they are in the self-harm early years, you really can't keep your eyes off of them for a moment. Taking turns with your spouse or caregiver is essential, as are getaways. Getaways can help to refresh and strengthen you, your spouse and your typically functioning child at least for awhile.

You may also consider asking your child to model good behaviors once in awhile for your autistic child. If Amalia wasn't terrified of small dogs, then she could have shown Josh how to pet one. Nevertheless, Amalia was fortunately Not afraid of going to the dentist. We asked to bring Josh in for one of her visits and Doctor Jon was very welcoming. Josh watched Amalia sit nicely in the chair, open her mouth, and even saw the instruments go into her mouth without any fear, because Amalia was calm. Because she modeled that task, Josh was then able to sit in a dental chair and have his teeth "counted" ever so slowly as the dentist checked them for cavities. Way to go Amalia, Sister of the year!

VACATIONS

Ira speaks as if in a dream of the day he never appreciated. He often reminds me of our honeymoon cruise through the Caribbean and the day he sipped Mango Mama's and read one book or another. He remembers that day very fondly and wishes that he had really appreciated it as it was occurring. Since that day we have taken several short family vacations to a variety of theme parks in Ohio, no Mango Mama's involved. Maybe an occasional super sweet smoothie or cotton candy. Here's what I have learned from our theme park outings, advice that I hope you will take to heart so as to avoid the several mistakes we initially made...

1. Make sure your hotel lobby is not crammed with sensory overload

There was one theme hotel we stayed at that had an arcade in the lobby and in every thoroughfare that we were forced to walk through each day. Other resorts have separate rooms for their arcades, but this hotel was one large walk through sensory hell for Josh and even for myself. It was as if we were transported to Vegas for kids. We couldn't get anywhere without going through the scary zone, and because of that reason, we will never go back to that hotel. Call in advance and ask what their particular layout is like, instead of just showing up hopeful like we did. We spent three hundred dollars a night, only to have to stay in the room a lot, to calm him down and help him feel better.

2. Try and get a suite instead of one room. If there's more people than just you and your child, then having a separate room is a wonderful choice, as it can be used as a time out room, or if someone needs a nap or quiet time away from others then there is a place to retreat and restore oneself. Parents, I'm not just talking about time out for your kids. You may

want to disappear in there as well for a spell…

If you go on-line a couple of months before your getaway, then there are often times massive discounts on suites. The earlier you book it, the cheaper it is I have found. And, a little effort now will make your stay much more enjoyable later. Also note that if money is currently an issue, then many of these fun waterparks and theme parks also have day passes which do not require an overnight stay.

Find a hotel that has restaurants within its walls. But avoid the Hibachi experience…. Perhaps. Our favorite choice in the Cedar Point area, in Sandusky, Ohio, is the Breaker's Hotel on the island. It has restaurants inside of a VERY large lobby. The building is over 100 years old and the hallway is absolutely massive with very high ceilings. No claustrophobia issues there. They also have an arcade hidden down one hall, and there are absolutely no arcade games strewn about the other space. The children's area of Cedar Pointe is within walking distance from the hotel, along a beautiful Great Lake view and there is a beach as well as swimming pools and a 1950's themed ice cream shop on the hotel premise. If you don't live near Ohio, just keep these ideas in mind when shopping for a vacation spot.

Oh, and if you do have a kitchen included in your suite, make sure that immediately upon entering the suite you find the knife block and hide it. Otherwise, your little sweetie might find it first. Always, above all else, I believe in safety first. There are too many unknowns in new environments. Why do I mention this? Because it is on my list of OH MY GOSH moments. Joshie found the knife block in our hotel suite, before we did. It was something I never imagined would be in a hotel room.

He walked up to me holding a large knife, not maliciously, but need I say more….? Had he approached Amalia first, it may not have gone so smoothly. CHECK YOUR ROOM THOROUGHLY…. And Un-plug your hotel phone from the wall, or you just may have room service, house cleaning and anyone else his little fingers decided to call, ringing your doorbell…

It is also nice to note, that if you are going to a theme park such as Cedar Point that you can register for a special pass to avoid lines if you have a special needs or handicapped child. Hey, there are some perks…

And to parents, please take heed of the following advice… I highly urge you to rest as much as you can before going on these trips, as they are anything but restful. You are always on alert, like a hawk, watching every step your kids take, and getting your lay of the land at the same time. I'm pretty certain that I slept fourteen hours the day after our two days there. But the trip isn't really for us. It's for the kids, so it's worth it. Take lots of pictures as well.

But again, avoid the Hibachi restaurant if you have a fire-phobe with you. I was feeling particularly brave on our last family outing to Cedar Pointe. We booked a beautiful Snoopy Suite at The Breakers hotel, in advance, and things were going so well once we arrived there, that I got a little too confident and decided to throw caution to the wind at dinnertime. Despite Joshua's scared wince at seeing a candle lit, or a fireplace in a television show, I somehow thought that eating at a Hibachi restaurant where they cook the food on the table in front of you would be a fantastic idea. Ira was doubtful, but I was in super confident mode and urged him to try, saying that we really should try and expand his venues and that today was going so well... Since Ira enjoys food so much, it wasn't much of a battle.

As soon as the table started steaming, Josh started screaming. Dinner was officially over before it began, irregardless of the eighty dollar bill we had already produced. We had to take turns watching Josh outside of the restaurant, where he peeked over the window to see the fire from a safe distance, as one of us ate. He was so upset that he even unnerved Amalia enough for her to leave as well. We were forced to abandon dinner number one, and to try the diner next door for dinner number two. The diner was a family country diner, directly next door to the Hibachi, which was far less expensive and pleasant, after we blew out the candle on its table...

I still believe that trying new things is important. Just do it when you're in a good place and try and have a sense of humor about it, if you can. Fortunately, the people in the restaurant after their initial shock at his scream, were rather amused at watching my husband and I take turns outside of the restaurant with Josh and Amalia as we waited for our dinners to be put into a carry-out box. As I sat at the table during my turn, I was urged by my fellow diners to order a drink. I swear they all would have ordered one for me had I not acquiesced. This time I didn't feel the tears approach at the pity, as it was far funnier than sad. The years soften the emotions.

I don't normally employ the "autism" card, but have learned that perhaps I should. When asked if we needed assistance while in line to Cedar Point amusement park, I said, Yes and please. I guess the line was too long, or there were just too many people, even though we were on the boardwalk and by the water, that Josh just couldn't stand to be there and was very vocal about it. A kind Cedar Point employee noticed us standing there looking stressed out with Josh screaming, and asked if we needed help. I told her that we would really appreciate early entry, as he has autism, and the large amount of people here are flipping him out. Within one minute, she returned with two elderly ladies who kindly escorted us to the gate, opened it for us, and there we were, the only non-employees to stand in Cedar Point, free of the masses of people previously surrounding us. It was amazing, and he calmed down immeasurably. We were even standing there waiting in peace while listening to the National Anthem, just the four of us in that park. The music didn't upset him, and being there alone really helped to start the day off right. It turns out that all of those people who were standing there waiting, were actually waiting for the large roller coasters, not the kids area anyway, so we had early entry, and when the park officially started, we were the only ones in the kids section for a good thirty minutes. He enjoyed the time so much that we actually lasted for two hours. If telling someone your child has Autism will help your child, then go for it. I won't be shy any longer.

HOLIDAYS

Ira has notoriously despised all holidays and birthdays which probably stems from his birth day being the day he lost his mother. If you really think about it, a child who is given away has a death experience very early in life. The sounds and smells of his mother of nine plus months just disappear, immediately. Within the six years before Ira proposed to me, there was a two year break-up until I returned to New York. After not seeing him for that long, I somehow still remembered that it was his birthday, and since I was in the area and in one of my spontaneously driven moods, I bought a slice of cheesecake, went to his apartment building and had the doorman call him. He was home, and up the elevator I went. He had grown a beard at that time I recall, and was alone on his birthday watching TV. We hadn't seen each other for two years since the day I left slamming the door behind me, in complete frustration with him. I said Happy Birthday, entered his apartment, and gave him the cake. He said, "Thanks, but I'm allergic to the strawberries on top." I told him to just eat the cheesecake then.

He had of course forgotten or tuned out the fact that it was his birthday, so he was shocked that I remembered. In the past fourteen years that we have been married, Ira has lightened up about birthdays and holidays, as he couldn't have married a more opposite person in this vein if he had tried. I LOVE decorating for all holidays, cooking, baking, inviting people over, throwing parties. I think we are the most opposite in so many respects, that it's really a miracle we are still together, especially with the percentage of people with an autistic child getting divorced at something like 90 percent. Irregardless, he has had to shift over to my side and leave the dark side as I like to call it. Though he still has the Star Wars Darth Vader theme as his

48

ring tone.... Now he does holidays.

Trick-or-Treating has also become a fun time to look forward to each year. However, it wasn't always that way. I used to be so nervous that Josh would run into the street, or that by taking him trick or treating, he would learn from us that it was all right to go up to stranger's doors and into their homes. Yes, every young child has to learn that it's not okay to run towards moving cars, or go into people's houses, but Josh is no longer a toddler, and sometimes it takes him a long time to learn social norms and what is right and what is not. I certainly did not want to be a source of confusion when it came to Halloween Trick-or-Treating, and it worried me quite a bit. Nevertheless, by explaining the rules to Josh and letting him know that this is only once a year, with mommy, daddy and big sister, as well as making it Very clear, in the Ultimate Serious, of serious tones, that he cannot run towards the street ever, then we were fine. Well, after a few mishaps.

Getting in front of the problem, in advance if possible, always seems to serve us best. However, though I prompted him in advance not to go anywhere near the street, but to stick to the grass, Josh did have a couple of times on our first Halloween walk around the block of about forty houses, that he started to run towards the street. When he did so, I was not shy. I used a loud harsh voice and caught up with him, stopped him, got on my knees, looked him in the face and said, "You are Never to run towards the street. Danger, Danger. Cars can hit you and make big ouchie." I then insisted he hold my hand for the next five houses, staying inside, closer to the houses than the street. After that, I told him, again on my knees, that I would let his hand go, if he Promises Not to run towards the street, because of dangerous cars. He said, "Okay", and that was a success.

The rest of our trick-or-treating was a lot of fun. The kids enjoyed themselves immensely, and after my internal fears were somewhat manifest, and I addressed them, and confidently believed he would not err again, then I even enjoyed myself as well.

Anything new with Josh is nerve racking, but the good news, is that once you do it, it's no longer new.... We have been trick-or-treating for three years now, and it is a joy. The kids look forward to it, they do not attempt to run into the street, and we have fun choosing costumes on e-bay, as the Halloween stores are simply too ghoulish and scary even for me. Prior to the big day we carve a happy pumpkin face, play the song "Monster Mash" about a dozen times, and decorate our home with pictures that are not evil or gross. On Halloween we go trick-or-treating, and pass out candy later, and it's guaranteed family fun each year.

BIRTHDAYS

Our Amalia, has had many wonderful, yet atypical birthday parties over the past nine years. She has had a dress-up as a princess party at our home, where all of the children were asked to wear dresses and we supplied princess props, as well as a visit from a Fairy Godmother in full costume with games ready. We have also rented out an English Tea restaurant, and invited the guests to come dressed up. Gloves and hats were provided to the little ladies as well as herbal teas and scones. Amalia has also had a Jungle party at a local Jungle Java venue where the kids could run around, climbing up the gargantuan jungle structure, sliding down a myriad of slides, swinging across zip lines and just having a fun time. All of her parties have been fantastic, and most importantly, all of them have included other children. She has invited at least twenty children to each party, except for the one year that she only had two friends of her choice to accompany her on a spa and cappuccino day. Decaf of course…

Alternatively, Joshua hasn't had the same experience. Each year until now, Josh has had a party at our home, with a meal, decorations, balloons and cake of course, but not at a venue, and not with other children invited. He has had relatives and perhaps one close friend only. Because of his autism, and my fear that he would not like the party due to some unforeseen sensory issue at a venue, as well as my fear that no friends would actually show, I had been very afraid to throw a large party and invite his school friends.

I am happy to say that this year was different. I think it is very important as I have said before, to trust your instincts, and sometimes it is also important to stay within your comfort zone until you are ready to do whatever it was that scared you. I am finally ready to throw Josh a party at a venue, with friends invited. The truth be told, I was scared that no one would come but for two friends. I know for certain that I am not alone in this feeling. Many parents who have children with special needs are afraid that their child will not have many friends. Josh has been very blessed to have at least two boys that he has play dates with every so often, and as of late, his teachers and paraprofessional's report that he is making more friends, particularly, children who are in the regular education classroom that he visits each day.

I sent out the twelve invitations very early and with trepidation, but determined to just get them out and to let the cards fall as they may... The teachers in the two autism classrooms were very supportive and happy to distribute the invites to Joshua's class with the older kids, and I also invited the younger newbies as well, which makes for eleven children plus two other friends from the Friendship Circle. No one RSVP'd for two weeks and I was nervous. I reasoned that it was early and waited patiently and hopefully. Then I heard from some mom's. They were the mother's of the newly autistic kids, the younger ones. They sounded so grateful that their son was invited and it clearly pained them to call me that it made me cry afterwards remembering how I felt such pain and gratitude the first time Josh was invited anywhere. I remember feeling thankful that someone would want him around, and then guilty for feeling like they were doing us a favor, because I love my son so much, that I felt I shouldn't feel that way. I felt so sorry and so much warmth towards them. I swear I'll probably hug them all when I meet them at his party in two weeks. "Thank you so much for inviting him." they sheepishly uttered. I replied with "Thank you so much for coming."

His teacher Miss Cathy suggested that I also invite some of his regular education friends, in particular, four children that have taken a liking to him and play with him on recess. I was conflicted. I wanted to, but was afraid of the rejection he might receive. Then I realized that Josh wouldn't even know if they were invited or not, and thus, if they were able to attend or not, so I sent some invitations to school for Cathy to distribute. Of the four regular education students we invited, one immediately responded that he will be there! I guess that had I chosen to protect Joshua and shelter him from rejection, that he wouldn't have had his amazing 8th birthday party. Again, it's about baby steps and comfort. When I was a walking crying basket case, a few years ago, I don't think I could have gotten it together to plan and throw him a party like this. But as time goes on, more things seem possible. Time really does heal and strengthen.

A worrisome thought that crossed my mind however was, "Does the mom of the regular education child even knows that Josh is on the spectrum?". When they arrive at the party and see a bunch of autistic kids there, will they feel uncomfortable? I hoped that it would still go as well as I'm envisioning, minus the negative thoughts... But really, what was I to do? Should I have written, Joshua's 8th Birthday (p.s. – he is in the Autism classroom and your son is kind to him and they play together)??? Why should I have to qualify who he is? I guess I just have to remember that the universe is in perfect order. If her son has not mentioned that Josh is in AI, then why should I....

Most ironically and synchronistically, only two hours after I sympathetically spoke with the mother's of the newbies responding, my little man came home with a birthday bowling party invitation in his backpack, from a child in his regular education inclusion class. I felt grateful, happy, and scared simultaneously. I didn't dare RSVP by phone, as I feared my emotions would get the best of me. I sent a text message instead and when the mom wrote back saying she was happy to have him, all I could write was, "Thanks so much" with heartfelt gratitude. I remember being in her place, feeling good about inviting the younger autistic newbies to Joshua's party and feeling overwhelming compassion for their mom's when I received their meek confirmations of attendance. Now I am in their shoes. What a roller coaster ride this has been.

The bowling birthday party held many wonderful surprises. Josh was one of fourteen children in attendance and the only child with special needs. We had never taken him bowling before, as we feared that he would become sensory overloaded with all of the noises and crowds in such a place, though we imagined that he would be a good bowler, as Josh has always been excellent with puzzles and excels visually and spatially. Temple Run on the I-pad is a treat that his teachers give to him each day after he finishes a certain amount of school work. He is able to jump and reroute the character on the I-Pad with ease. Perhaps that is also why he is so adept at bowling! Josh was on the birthday boys team, and out of all of the kids there, he bowled the highest score of one hundred and two, the first time he ever played. Kids and parents were astounded and cheered him on. He threw the ball and walked away to sit before watching the progress of his throw, in a very Sheldon Big Bang Theory kind of a way.

The first four frames he got spares. The first four he ever played! He even helped the birthday boy to ultimately win the game because of his skill and score. It tickles me to think that Josh was not a burden on the party and guests, but instead their hero. Before I was just so grateful to have him invited. Now he is an esteemed comrade and valued player. The Autistic boy saved the day!! Yay Josh, Bravo!!!

Amalia is also very adept at bowling, so perhaps this will become a weekly event. Josh keeps asking, "Wanna go to da bowling pen". I think he thinks it's a pen because they call them bowling pins. He can call it whatever he wishes. And we will most certainly indulge this interest.

Fast forward after Joshua's most successful birthday party yet! We had a total of fifteen children show up at his eighth birthday. Not that I'm counting, okay, maybe I am, but that is actually more kids at his party than at the typically functioning child's bowling party. I guess my fear was unfounded.

So fifteen children showed up and had free and organized play in the Gym area with two instructors on hand to help them. They had such a fun time, and there were typical children playing with our special needs ones on the spectrum. It was so different than what I remembered growing up in the nineteen seventies. I remember children being Really quite mean to the special needs students. I had also feared it would still occur in 2013 and that no one from the regular class would even show.

One of the boys at his party from his inclusion, regular education class actually said, "Josh is my very best friend. But is he British?" No kid, he's dyspraxic, but I'll take British. How cute! Everyone played well and truly the only issue we had was when my thirty-four year old brother Mike who is six feet plus tall decided it would be fun to throw balls at the kids. He really didn't have any evil intentions, just thought they'd like it, and they did, until he nailed one of them a little too hard. He was the only "Kid" there that received a time out that day...

When it came to cake and candle time we lit the candles with trepidation as Josh has a fire phobia. He instantly pushed his seat back about 3 feet. The manager of the venue said, "Wow, I wish all the kids were that smart". Warm and fuzzy again.

INDOOR PETS, OUTDOOR PETS, AND OH NO, QUICK DETOUR, THERE'S SOMEBODY ELSE'S PET

Before you judge our choices you must listen to the entire story. Ira and I were such avid animal lovers, that when we lived in New York City, BK, Before Kids, we were the loving caregivers to 4 parakeets who all were allowed to fly freely in our studio apartment, then retire to their "home", not cage, we didn't want them to feel constricted, whenever they wished. We also cared for what started as two dwarf hamster's and rapidly turned into a tribe with at least a dozen furless babies running around their house at any given time. We were creative and space efficient enough to add a terrarium with frogs as well as a heated "home" for our spotted Gecko named Sydney. We cared for these animals in five hundred and eighty square feet of space, virtually one room, with a bathroom, and they were not only well fed and kept clean, but they were loved as well.

If it were not for my allergies, I would be thrilled to have a dog and a cat. Unfortunately, we never were able to have those two types of pets. Or, maybe it actually was good fortune, as the dog and cat probably wouldn't have worked out very well with our other pets at snack time. Irregardless, we love animals and several years later, we continue to love and care for them.

Then along came Joshua…. We currently have three Orange fan-tailed Oranda Goldfish who are each the size of my hand. Two of our fish are already about five years old each and they live in our one hundred gallon tank that spans half of our kitchen wall. The other fish is also of the same variety and lives in a more humble twenty gallon tank in our family room

54

area. Apparently we have a thing for orange, as our other pet is an orange canary of the male variety, whom the kids named "Orange". He's a boy and thus a wonderful singer which is characteristic of the male canary. He also lives in the family room in his "house".

Outside, in our backyard area, we daily feed our large variety of birds, which Amalia now recognizes by name. We have cardinals, blue jays, woodpeckers, sparrows, finches, goldfinches, black birds, turtle doves, hummingbirds and also hawks visit daily. The hawks don't eat the seed, they eat the other birds when they can. Circle of life stuff. We are also visited weekly by deer, foxes, opossums and raccoons at night, squirrels, chipmunks, cats, bunnies, mice and groundhogs daily. They too enjoy the seed as well as apples from our trees. It is a very calming scene to just sit by the window on the couch and stare outside. You never know who will visit, and they are all gorgeous and fascinating creatures.

The kids also enjoy this pastime, and even when a large male deer comes by, antlers and all, Josh has learned to show respect and to sit quietly and just watch. There have been times when the male deer, never the female, will challenge us with a stare, and we have all learned to bow our heads and allow him dominion lest he charge the window. He will then go back to peacefully eating the seed we left for him, only five feet away from the window we are sitting by. There was even one time that I dared to go outside when the seeds were gone, to replenish their supply. I went straight up to the female deer, head lowered, and she accepted my offering of food, then I backed away. In other words, the kids are not afraid of a small horse sized animal with threatening antlers. They are accustomed to our indoor and outdoor pets.

Not so lucky when it comes to dogs however... I cannot pinpoint where this started, or why, but both of our children are terrified of small dogs. Not the large dogs like our neighbor Ram walks around our block daily. Yes, they have natural trepidation about approaching Snowy, a large gorgeous Samoyeds, but will still approach because of their familiarity with he and Ram. And, they jump for joy when they see Skylar outside next door as well. Skylar is our German Shepherd mixed friend whom they play with sometimes throughout the summer. However, if we take a walk around the block and there is a tiny little Shih tzu, the blood curdling screams that emerge from Josh are potentially deafening.

One time over the summer we took a family walk to our community pond, only five minutes away in our sub-division to feed the Geese. Now if you know anything about animals, you know that Geese can be very vocal and confrontational. They will hiss at you, run after you, and even try and bite you if you rub them the wrong way or simply walk too close to them or their young. The kids know that and will show the Geese and Swans great respect. We bring bread and feed them, even daring to get rather close to them at times, heads bowed of course. If Josh is a little abrupt and a Goose feels threatened and starts hissing and flapping at him, he will laugh a little and back up with me, to give them some room. There is no drama, no blood curdling-deafness inducing screams… He just backs up.

Unfortunately, on the way home from the pond, we had the misfortune of passing two tiny little dogs sitting on their property. Josh absolutely went into panic mode. He was beyond upset. He was truly terrified. They were outside on their lawn, fenced in by an invisible fence, which may have been the problem. In Joshua's mind, he may have thought that they were free to attack him. We have had similar reactions from Josh during walks at Farmer's Markets in the summer when he sees a small dog, but never as upset as with those two leash-less ones. He actually climbed my body, screaming all the while, as I reassured him they wouldn't attack. That didn't serve to calm him in the least, and so I simply just started running with him to get some distance between us and the dogs so that he could see they weren't following. He finally calmed down, but I couldn't imagine that we were going to go petting small dogs anytime soon.

Ironically a week later he fed large goats and sheep at a petting zoo. Perhaps the higher pitched barking of the smaller dogs also hurts his brain, like a siren would. So if you are considering adding a pet to your family, I highly urge you to take baby steps, and see if your child's reaction will be one that is positive, neutral, negative, or OMG negative. My goal for Josh is to go from OMG negative, to just negative. So I just bought him a small robotic furry dog that yaps and jumps. Maybe one day we'll get to neutral…

And thankfully that day did occur. Writing this book has been a very emotional process. I have fought writing it almost every step of the way, as I can't help but to cry every time I sit down and remember all of these stories. As I re-read I am amazed, as you will be for yourselves should you take notes on your situation, that only six months after writing about the two dogs that Josh was so truly terrified of, he has recovered from his small dog phobia.

We visited a local PetSmart store, despite the fact that dogs are allowed to roam about with their owners. Even seeing a small dog within fifty feet used to be enough to set him off. Nine week old Beagle mixed Rocky was roaming about with his owner, and so I started to redirect Josh so that we would not be at all near him, but Josh surprised me with different plans. He said, "Pet dog". I thought he meant that the dog was someone's pet, as I couldn't fathom the possibility that he was using the word "pet" as a verb. When I finally realized what he was asking, I very meekly, with great trepidation, approached the dog's owner and asked about her puppy. She said he was sweet and that Josh could pet him if he'd like to. Josh was determined, and though his body leaned in the opposite direction, his feet kept moving him forward. I knelt down and pet Rocky first, after allowing the puppy to smell my hand. Josh decided that a rear end approach would be better, but it wasn't comfortable to the dog to have a strange boy approach him from behind, so I gently urged Josh to kneel beside me, demonstrating confidence all the while as I pet Rocky. Not only did he pet him once, but he did so twice. I could barely hold my tears back. Another milestone was met.

If you do decide to add a pet to your lives, please consider enforcing rules from the outset that are very clear to your child. Josh doesn't yet have a good grasp of gray areas. He understands never touch this, but if he sees the rule broken once, then we're in for quite a battle, and for a long time. So when we brought Orange our canary home, I spoke privately with Amalia and then with both of them together, and made them both promise to Never touch the cage-house. I let Amalia know that she needs to respect this completely, because I am certain, from much experience, that if she even casually touched the cage, that Josh would then think he had free license to not only touch it, but to carry it to his room, endangering Orange, if he fancied a canary visit. Josh really requires absolutes in this realm, and with safety issues as well. Consider your own child. Can you think of anything that you require absolute obedience on? If so, consider making that clear immediately so that negative habits do not form.

SAFETY FIRST

There are rules that are non-negotiable and serious in our lives. For example, when Halloween trick-or-treating each year, we Must stay on the grass since there are no sidewalks in our neighborhood. In the earlier years of Joshua's life when he was learning about how to be safe walking to feed the Geese at our sub-division pond, we would actually stop walking the moment we heard a car coming by and back up even further onto the grass. I would say "cars in street can be dangerous. Let's look and wait until they leave and then we can go". It must have looked ridiculous to all of our neighbors passing by, but I felt very firmly that since he had originally no understanding about the dangers of a car, that we had to step it up even higher.

One day before we had moved to our home, we lived in a condominium which was secured with an alarm. I was in the bathroom, going to the bathroom, when I heard a loud beep, which sounded like a door alert going off. I wasn't expecting Ira home, and so I jumped up and practically fell over my pants as I ran to see what was going on. Amalia, who was only about four years old at that time, just pointed to the front door which was ajar. Josh had managed to open the door at age three, and to run outside into the street in front of our condo. I of course ran, barefoot and half dressed out the door after him. He was three condominiums away in a diaper, not potty trained at the time, barefoot and only wearing a shirt. He was laughing and running, looking back at me and laughing even more. I was screaming stop, come back etc....I finally caught up to him, picked him up and carried him home saying in a very firm voice. "No go street. Danger." I would often Purposefully omit words such as "the" or "in", as he was still working to gain receptive language, and I believed that using even contractions such as "Don't" for "Don't go into the street", would

58

only slow his learning curve down. So oftentimes sentences became shortened, such as "No Go Street!". If your child is in the pre-verbal stages, try shortening the sentences. They will probably learn to understand faster with less. Josh did.

An hour later Ira came home with chain locks and installed them at the very top of each door to the outside, as well as bars on the top of door walls. Joshua had absolutely zero concept that cars could hurt him, that he was potentially in danger, and that he should be careful. Now granted he was only three years old at the time, but I was not willing to take a chance with him, so our safety lessons began shortly thereafter.

The Friendship Circle I mentioned earlier, actually has a person dressed like a policeman in the section where the traffic lights are in the safety training area. Kids can ride a tricycle around the street, but Must obey the traffic rules. At first Ira would allow Josh to ride his bike in the wrong direction, and on the sidewalks, actually laughing at his defiance, and we had a few fights about that, but Josh now really understands that he must follow safety rules. I think however that I may have taken it a bit far, because now when we are driving and I turn left on a blinking red light, Josh will scream "NO Mommy!" Red Light STOP!" I have tried to explain that it is okay if the red light is blinking, but he just gets upset and says "I not like you mommy. You need time out." I figure that its better he has a clue about rules and follows them, even strictly, than to just walk into the street obliviously.

Nowadays when we walk to feed the Geese, he will yell at Ira to stand on the grass as well, which I find completely loving and sweet as it demonstrates his love for all of us. Or perhaps it is a little Obsessive Compulsive as well, in that he often times wants us all to do exactly what he is doing. Either way, it works with safety issues.

Joshua is still in the Autism Program at school, and so he rides a special needs bus, driven by a saint called, Miss Annie. Miss Annie picks him up at our house, unlike the regular education buses which have assigned stops for each neighborhood, not door to door service. We are so blessed to have someone like Miss Annie. Not all bus drivers have heart and in fact his last driver did not like driving the special needs bus and asked for a transfer, which was great for all of us, as I saw her behaving aggressively towards him, picking him up with impatience not heart, as she strapped him in. Miss Annie is the best, and I hope that your bus driver is too. She even pulls the bus over puddles so that he stays dry. Every person who interacts with your child has some kind of influence on them. I never forget that, and always make it my business to know them as well as I can.

This morning as Josh waited for his bus, Ram walked by again with beautiful Snowy. He and Snowy will visit periodically and Josh looks forward to seeing them. Unfortunately, it was a cold and slippery snowy day outside, and so naturally Ram didn't want to walk up the driveway as we have a bit of a hill and he could have slipped. If Josh were to spend any time with Snowy, which he likes to do nowadays, then he would have to walk past our pre-assigned safety zone part of the driveway and into the NO GO zone, close to the street. I immediately put a stop to Josh passing the safety line, and was met with his very upset protest via screams and whines and he was very close to throwing himself on the ground in a tantrum, but didn't want to risk getting wet. I asked Ram and pup to ascend the driveway, but instead of approaching Josh due to their fear of slipping, they just stood there. This detente created tension for Joshua and Ira just politely asked them to visit another time.

I know with certainty, that had we allowed Josh to pass the line before the bus had arrived and stopped, then we would be opening the doorway for him to do so whenever he wished, a slippery slope both literally and figuratively. He would most likely even then consider pushing the envelope further and venturing forth into the street, which of course is not safe. Drivers nowadays are just not as careful as they used to be, as they reach for their telephones to text people or check messages as they rush to work, and so both Ira and I in the moment decided to keep the restriction strict, and even risk offending our well-liked neighbor. I did text Ram later to explain why we were short with him and he was not offended after all. Children on the spectrum do not do well when rules are broken or bent. They need absolutes and firm rules on safety issues. The firmness of the rules creates order for them and the whole family, plus it can make the difference between safety and disaster.

VIDEO GAMES

The first time we encountered video games in abundance was as I mentioned at a resort that we stayed at, and because of the video games and how loud they were, and the fact that they were in every area you were forced to walk through, we will not choose to stay at that particular resort again. However, now that we've spent some time at a different resort that had a small arcade (in a hidden area of the hotel) and we discovered the magic of the motorcycle game, our perspective has shifted.

I am definitely not an advocate of sitting children in front of a television or video games to keep them busy. In fact, I won a Nintendo DS system at a local country club Bingo that I was a guest at, and I promptly gave it to the hostess who invited me and told her she could borrow it for a year.

As the children became older and we took more road trips, I asked for that system to be returned for the express purpose of road trip usage ONLY. It helped a lot with long drives and the kids also had to learn how to take turns and to be patient when it wasn't their turn. Unfortunately, Josh only enjoyed Killing Chickens on the Zelda game, and didn't understand how to play it in a traditional manner, so when I saw him taking too much pleasure in killing the chickens, I found games that didn't allow you to kill anything other than robots.

When we were staying at the resort with the motorcycle game, the kids spent much of their day on the beach, or at the amusement park, playing and having good solid physical activity and fresh air socialization time. So, spending thirty minutes in the arcade later in the day didn't feel distasteful to me, like a wrong choice. They both gravitated to the motorcycle riding game and were both excellent at it. Josh literally leaned so far left that he

61

was almost falling off of the bike, but his scores were excellent on the game, and he was clearly having fun. Again, a spatial capability.

So when we returned from our trip I had it in my mind to get them a system for in home use. We brought home a 3D system that is very commonly used nowadays, and I tried it out and within about fifteen minutes I felt dizzy, a headache was also forming, and I became disoriented. I actually read the box of the system and it warned that it could cause neurological problems, so I promptly repackaged the game, grabbed the receipt and returned it in time before the kids even got home from school. I wholeheartedly believe that so many things in our world today are harming us, and we may not even know it for fifty years from now.

So how could I simulate their fun experience on the 2D motorcycle game? I thought back on my own childhood in the 1980's and how I used to play all sorts of wonderful games, that didn't make me feel nauseated. I fondly recall playing word story games on the green screen of the Apple II computer that prompted you to write two word commands such as "Go North" or "Grab watch". Unfortunately, those games wouldn't do, as Josh wasn't yet up to that reading level. So I continued to reminisce and thought of Atari and Space Invaders, Nintendo NES, Zelda and Donkey Kong, Super Mario Brothers and others, and thus my E-bay search began. I found a Nintendo NES original gaming system with controllers and several games for sale on E-bay. I purchased the system, and about six days later we plugged it in. Other than having to literally blow on the game before inserting it, it works perfectly. I put Super Mario Brothers and Zelda in to check them out and see if I would become ill or not, and of course to enjoy the nostalgia of just even seeing these games, some twenty plus years later. What a fun time it was for me, and thankfully, 2D does not give me any illnesses. I figured that if I was bothered by 3D that it simply could not be good for the kids, even if they exhibit zero negative side affects. So the next problem to overcome was how in the world would I keep Josh from becoming obsessed with this game and demanding it twenty four hours, seven days a week? And even more importantly, how would I get him to share and give Amalia a turn?

What a WONDERFUL thing the 2 player feature is!!! This feature allows two people to play the same game and to take turns, mandated by the computer, and not me. You get out, then you have to wait for the other person to lose. Josh didn't like waiting, but all I could do was point back to the machine. That's how it works buddy. You play, you get out, its Amalia's turn, she gets out, then it's your turn again. He couldn't be mad at me, or at Amalia for having to wait. What a blessing! It turns out that they both really enjoy playing Super Mario Brothers, as much as I did as a child, and so we now find our family in the playroom playing games, and taking turns in what appears to be a normal, typically functioning family. Josh is not having tantrums about taking a turn, and Fully accepts the paradigm. It almost feels like a miracle.

When we play Board games, such as Life, or Sorry, he is not nearly as good about waiting for his turn. I really believe that because the computer is in charge it makes all the difference for us, in a really positive sense. And since we have had success with Super Mario Brothers, I found a matching game that features the Super Mario Brother characters. He Loves it! It's a simple matching game, and he waits patiently for his turn. The other day we all got a really good laugh when Josh said to Amalia as she was trying to recall where a match would be, "It's not happening Nalia.... My turn." And now Josh is creating his own matching games, drawing figures of the Mario characters in pairs, completely unprompted.

The other wonderful change that we are benefiting from thanks to this new found love, is that I can use the game system to get him to do homework. Homework is a new task for us. For many years Joshua had none. At the latest IEP meeting I requested he start to receive homework. Wow, did they take me up on it. At one point I had forty pages that were stapled together in packets and Josh was only barely finishing one page per day.

Not anymore... So happy to report that since Josh really enjoys playing Super Mario Brothers, that I have a bargaining tool now that I did not have before. Each time I have some homework for him to do, I will allow him to start to play the game, and about twenty minutes in, after his game has ended (doing this respectfully), I will turn the picture off on the television, and tell him its homework time, and that he can play after he finishes two or three pages. I will give him a specific number, and decide in advance based on the complexity of the assignment. If the homework seems simple, then I will expect we do three pages. If not, then two is enough.

Each time we have begun the homework Josh verbally resists and tries to convince me to change my mind by kissing me and looking cute and saying "Play game with me mommy", or by all out tears and screams of "NO homework!". His cute and obnoxious ways no longer deter me and I stick to my original plan. I have found that once we get through about thirty seconds of doing the work that the resistance disappears entirely. Basically, he realizes that I mean business and that he might as well get it over with as soon as possible, and not drag it out, so that he can get back to his beloved game.

We have always had a tough time with transitions with Joshua. However, thirty seconds is barely noticeable. There were times in the past that he would carry on for hours. As he has gotten older and has learned that we really will honor what we promise him, his whine time has decreased substantially. Once he does what is necessary, whether it be opening your mouth for the doctor, or doing homework, then we give him exactly what we promised, and promptly. Homework time is now done with ease and I am even feeling confident enough with him to insist that he erase letters that don't look very clear and that he write them again. In the past I would have been terrified of his response to that request, so much so, that I would just get the bare minimum out of him. Nowadays I see that he is so much more capable of doing so much more, and that not insisting more out of him is in actuality, irresponsible parenting. I also believe that I have gained confidence and view higher expectations and discipline as loving, not evil or mean.

REGRESSIONS - THE INFAMOUS "R" WORD

Another scary word that is commonly used in the Autism world is Regression. The Merriam-Webster on-line dictionary defines "Regression" as: 1. the act or an instance of regressing 2. a trend or shift toward a lower or less perfect state: as   a. progressive decline of a manifestation of disease b(1) : gradual loss of differentiation and function by a body part especially as a physiological change accompanying aging   (2) : gradual loss of memories and acquired skills c : reversion to an earlier mental or behavioral level d : a functional relationship between two or more correlated variables that is often empirically determined by data and is used especially to predict values of one variable when given values of the others <the regressions of y on x is linear|>; specifically : a function that yields the mean value of a random variable under the condition that one or more independent variables have specified values 3 : retrograde motion.

The closest definition for our purposes would be "C". "Reversion to an earlier mental or behavioral level. As I mentioned earlier, regressions are typical on this journey, though that knowledge doesn't make them easier on the child or people who love him. I remember feeling perpetually concerned that his three steps backward would leave him backwards with no future gain. I was almost completely unable at various times in our autism journey to see any positive outcome. Those moments were very fortunately, short-lived, but easy to recall due to the depth of their feeling. I was worried, terribly worried that his back steps would only lead to more of a regression. However, most fortunately in Joshua's case we have found that with a regression a giant leap follows. Sometimes it takes a couple of weeks, but like clockwork there has always been a positive milestone achieved in the end. I believe, have witnessed and have heard many other experts theorize that the child may regress in order to acclimate new

65

information or skills. Thankfully Joshua fits into that category, and your child most likely will as well. I think of it sometimes like a physical workout. The body will be very sore for awhile as well as uncooperative, but will come out stronger after the pain subsides.

Of course, a regression for a toddler or younger child on the spectrum is more terrifying for several reasons, one reason being that you have very little history of success to turn to during the rough times. I can now look back and say "Yes, My son can go to the bathroom by himself. He can speak and understand most everything we are saying, and he can even read and write many, many words." However, when Joshua was a toddler and had a regression, his regressions made us fear he would never be able to implement any of his newly acquired skills, simply because we hadn't seen any success and of course, many professionals will be quick to point out that forty percent of autistic people never speak. How sad that is to hear and how defeating if you let it be. Though I went through many a pity party, I never gave up hope that Josh would succeed. No matter what you do or how you feel, Please never give up hoping that your child will be in the sixty percent of autistic people who do speak, even when speech therapists seem reticent to encourage your hope. I used to ask people what they thought, and often times they would just say, "I can't say." That was always a blow to my outlook, until one day I decided that I wouldn't put any weight on their response. I would look at the odds, and keep believing, and by the way, six out of ten is in fact pretty good odds.

We just experienced another regression over Thanksgiving vacation. It's true that most people on the spectrum thrive on schedules and predictability, and our Thanksgiving vacation offered none of the above, with the added bonus of a sensory overloaded week and company. Our house is fairly large, but add six more people to the mix, and that's overwhelming for anyone, let alone Josh. Part of why we left New York was due to the small apartment we lived in and the overcrowding of the city.

I can even recall having people over our first Michigan residence, which was double the space of our New York apartment, only to have Josh go into full meltdown and scream until they made an early exit. So although he can tolerate company far better than he used to, it makes sense that Josh had a regression over Thanksgiving, as people on the spectrum must work harder to live in this sensory overloaded world than someone without the disorder. It's more difficult for them because some days they are hyper-sensitive to sounds, lights, touch or people, whereas on other days they are under-sensitive. There's nothing predictable about that to them, and it just depends on how their body is reacting. In order to help them we can become more sensitive to the surroundings we create for them at home, and where we take them. I have learned that Joshua really does not like to be in a mall or sports stadium, and so I wont take him there. Why expose him to something that may set him off into sensory overload?

Joshua knew we were having company later that day, and kept asking when they were coming. We told him after lunch, but that did not stop the queries. In retrospect, we learned not to tell Joshua about a party that he is excited to have, until an hour beforehand, as he just couldn't understand that he had to wait and that set him up to feel anxious all day, and to drive us a bit crazy too. He must have asked over one thousand times when they would all arrive. Nothing calmed him, and though we answered him each time, he still asked. Perhaps he thought that we would change our answer, or perhaps he just didn't understand the concept of time well enough to log the information and to find something else to do in the meantime. I offered lots of different activities, but he was stuck. Nevertheless, the party finally started as family members arrived.

One of the six additional people in our home was his cousin Joe, a beautiful baby who naturally would periodically cry or coo loudly. However, Josh seemed out of sorts, probably from his anxiety and questioning us all day long, and he actually put his hands over his ears like he used to do several years ago and said, "Too loud". It was very sad to see and sort of broke our hearts all over again. I ended up holding him upstairs in his room as if he were a baby, and he pretended to be a baby. Makes me cry even writing it now. He had regressed. The following week he continued to behave in a sensory overloaded fashion.

Fortunately, as I explained before, we have experienced so many giant leaps after regressions, that I found myself in detective mode yet again. His regression forced me to look around and see what I could possibly change or do to help him through this. I realized so many wonderful things that I immediately began to fix. I normally do not call his doctor. For me, considering that our son became autistic after the MMR shot, it is very difficult to count on modern medicine. Nevertheless, over the past three months Josh had been coughing enough to have us bring him to the doctor three times, once a month. Each time his doctor said it was allergies. Josh was prescribed an allergy medication, and it did help at first. We were also told that it is a very high allergy season this year, even into October and November. Well, December just rolled around, and that explanation was gnawing at my conscience and so I called our very kind doctor and we spoke for awhile and realized that his allergies have coincided with two things. One, we have our new bird, Orange. Doctor Bobby told us that they are very big triggers for allergies. Also, for school each day, we used to make a full cooked meal for Josh which consisted rather steadily, of pasta with olive oil and salt, ham cut into four sliced squares, sautéed broccoli, a banana, and a one hundred percent juice, berry juice. However, Joshua's friends were all ordering lunch at school, and his teachers told us that he seemed interested in joining them and ordering, and so we stopped cooking his homemade lunches and allowed him to eat the school lunches for the past three months. We also discovered two large stuffed animal snowmen were moved by Joshie right next to his bed. I moved them out of there because I thought they might have dust mites that bothered him. Not only did they have dust mites, but I realized that they were an estate sale find, and that I started sneezing once I picked them up. The home they were from was a nice and clean one, but I recalled a large dog there, and so our detective work paid off.

Doctor Bobby and I both discovered a total of three potential reasons for his coughing and allergies, which most likely also caused him to regress. It could have been either the bird, the school food, or the estate sale stuffed animal finds. Perhaps his regression is not so much a regression as it is him just feeling crabby and cranky and not wanting to be around people because of it. Of course that doesn't account for his asking us the same question approximately one thousand times, but it could be contributory. Bottom line is that if you are seeing a regression, sit down, get quiet, and go over EVERYTHING in your mind from his bedroom environment, to the home, his school, his health, what he's eating, etc… and you will undoubtedly come across something you may have overlooked. I practically kicked myself for not realizing sooner that the stuffed snowmen were full of dog hair, but beating yourself up isn't going to do any good for you or your child, so try and just plough forward and do better next time. At least that's what I told myself. Well, after I stopped beating myself up for the miss I moved forward.

Someone once pointed out to me that we never know what life will bring. That a typically functioning child, even the quarterback of the high school football team, in top physical condition, may one day most unfortunately be involved in an accident that leaves him in a state of extreme regression and even physical limitation. I believe that they told me that to help me. In a way it did, as it made me appreciate that my boy wasn't that boy, and that each day we could work to help him become better, not unlike the former football player receiving rehabilitation services. Perhaps pondering this thought which is innately a scary thought will help you to realize as well, that life just happens, and that we have two choices. We can complain about it and stay defeated, or we can make the more growth filled choice which is to embrace the circumstance wholeheartedly and do everything we are capable of doing to improve it.

RESPITE

For the longest time I was under the impression that I was the only person fit, loving and knowledgeable enough to care for our children. I wouldn't even leave them with Ira until their heads were hardened enough for him not to accidentally cause them injury. In fact, I remember waking up at five am when we lived in New York City, so that I could sneak out while they were sleeping and be back before they awoke. I would walk to the Starbucks at Seventieth and Amsterdam Avenue where it connects to Broadway and sit there so very grateful to have alone time, sipping a non-fat latte and reading inspiring materials.

Now that the children are older, and I am more comfortable because their skulls have hardened and they can walk and understand important safety information, I will leave them with Ira when necessary, and have hired a babysitter, Bela Mittelman, who is a huge blessing to our family, and has been with us for five years now. For the first several months when Bela started, I would stay with her to show her the ropes and to feel confident enough to leave her with them. It was a brilliant idea that I had read somewhere, and if you can afford to do so, then I highly urge you to start training someone to care for your child and give yourself a few hours a week for respite. Ira and I have one date night and one date day per week. With the divorce statistics as high as they are, we are very conscious about creating adult time. Last I checked, the divorce rate for couples with a child on the spectrum, was at ninety percent. Not the bad enough fifty percent. No, ninety percent. Please remember that it may not be necessary for you to leave your marriage. You may just need some respite. If you cannot currently afford a babysitter, then try and get grand-parents, friends or siblings to do even an hour. Every little bit of time alone helps strengthen you, and strong mommy's and daddy's equals happier children and safer and stronger marriages.

We are also so grateful for the teenage volunteers who through the friendship circle have visited our house for one to two hours, once a week, practically every week of the year. These teenagers volunteer out of the goodness of their hearts and when you find a fun, engaging volunteer that your child looks forward to seeing, you have really hit the jackpot. Joshua currently has one such person. Her name is Courtney Pefley and she is a true blessing to us. Joshua looks forward to seeing her each week and we know that if it is a Courtney day, that it is a better day for all of us. Gina Bryant, Courtney's friend also joined us on Sunday's for Amalia, and it is a good day when I know they are coming. I have heard about many programs in different counties across the United States which have similar respite programs with their own volunteers. Ask your school, or look it up on the web. As Jenny McCarthy wrote in her book about her son Evan, "Google it". You may also consider going to your local church or religious institution for ideas and or aid.

I was sitting in church a few weeks ago when a picture was presented above us of a young boy and his mother. The woman speaking said that they had called for help. Before she even mentioned what kind of help it was that they required, I whispered to my friend, "That child has Autism. You can see it in his smile. I'm probably going to cry soon." Lo and behold the child was Autistic and Dyspraxic, and his mom was seeking financial assistance to help house them here in Michigan for the duration of their very expensive speech therapy. Her church representative from the southern state they lived in, happened to call our church on an intuition. People typically do want to help others in need, so don't be shy. Request away, but make sure you can trust the ones you are seeking help from, certainly if you are going to leave your child in someone else's care.

I was more than reluctant at first to allow anyone else to care for my babies, but I knew when I had found the right person, and I spent five months with her training her, and so I felt completely comfortable when I did decide to go out that first time. So glad that I gave it a chance. There are gifts that Bela, Courtney and Gina bring to the table that I just do not possess, and so Joshua and Amalia are both being enriched by their presence. And so am I.

FULL CIRCLE

Every person I meet and discuss Autism with has an opinion on what we should do. Well, at least that was how it was for a few years. Now that Josh is successfully recovering and exhibiting far more typical behaviors than Autistic ones, the advice has slowed down quite a bit. Nevertheless, when we took Josh out of the esteemed speech therapy that was behaviorally focused several years ago when his speech therapist told me I was no longer allowed in the room with him, I had a backlash from many people who insisted that I was making a mistake. They would remind me after all, that this is one of the top centers for dyspraxia and autism related speech disorders in the country.

Being a conscientious mom, I had to consider their words, and the fact that this speech therapy facility was ranked rather highly, but as I considered, I also kept reminding myself that I was in fact acting on his behalf in the best way at the time. Replaying the therapists words, "We have to break him like a horse" seemed to help allay my fear and insecurities that I had made a mistake. Their approach just felt inhumane. When I met with the director of the program, who I had been in a community theatre show with years before, she was very belligerent with me for even questioning her esteemed program, and we parted with bad feelings. I have never returned to this day, and am retrospectively grateful for that choice.

At a party I was seated by a woman I had never before met. We became engrossed in a discussion about Autism, as she is a special education teacher. She shared her sadness for the children she sees who are put through stringent behavioral therapies, and how inhumane they can be. She mentioned that more people were being coerced into bringing their children to the ABA programs, as insurance is now covering them for that modality alone, at least in Michigan. I shared my ABA experiences with her both from the perspective of having been a full time teacher to the boy in New York and seeing him go through various behavioral sessions, as well as what I had experienced with Josh. From hearing her stories, I can now see that we really did make the best choice for Joshua. So many kids are stifled from growing into their true personalities and from being happy go lucky children, as they are forced into these ABA programs that "break them". It was a nice reminder that trusting my instincts is always the best thing to do even if others disapprove. This reminder is helpful even years later. Josh is the happiest child around and now that he has receptive language, we do use some behavioral therapy techniques, but not in a cruel way. I am so happy that people are treating the Autistic child and person with more dignity than what I have seen in the ABA program and philosophy, at least of the ones I have personally witnessed.

It is also heartbreaking to hear about children who have been through that program and turn out to be very angry and rebellious as a response to the constant demoralization and stringency. I have learned that many parents who are stressed out by their child's negative behaviors choose to medicate these children to deal with their anger instead of addressing it and helping them in a natural way. There are many over-medicated children out there who just need to feel respected and who also need to be given some autonomy over their lives, real or imagined. If you can offer your child two options, Mac and cheese or hot dogs, then that is a step towards respecting them and granting them some power and control over their lives which is what I believe is lacking.

I have witnessed one particular child who is a product of ABA and over-medication, and each time I see him I notice the vast difference between he and Josh. Josh is well-behaved and plays well, meaning that he engages appropriately, isn't destructive in his play or aggressive. This other boy is constantly upset or trying to cause some kind of drama or acts in a deviant manner in play, and in front of his parents, I think on purpose. I believe he does so in order to show them that he is somewhat in charge, even if that means he will be in trouble later. He is staging protests dozens of times a day in an attempt to gain some control over his life which has not been his in very many empowering a way. His behaviors have included spitting, pushing people, punching, swearing and hitting. Now verbal, he threatens attacks on others in very scary fashions. His well intentioned parents decided to put him on several different mood altering drugs to control his behaviors. Very sad indeed. What is worse, is that medical professionals will push the idea of drugging your child in lieu of working with him in alternate ways such as play therapy or just good old fashioned fun. Just remember who you are speaking with. If you go to a psychiatrist, expect drugs to be pushed. That's what they do. A surgeon will want to do surgery. A therapist will want to listen, a behavioral therapist will want to set up plans to change behaviors. Who you go to will determine where you may be headed unless you are strong enough to resist their offers of solutions. As I mentioned before, we do not medicate Josh except for a pro-biotic, which is akin to a vitamin on some level. It doesn't alter his mood or change his personality. It simply aids his stomach in digestion. Please don't let people push you into unnecessary treatments because they have a PhD or MD title after their name. Be strong for your child and know when to say NO. We did, and though we had many people judging us, we are certainly glad we said no, as it has made all the difference.

I recall working as a camp counselor when I was a teenager. There was one child at the camp who was really hyper-active and always had a twinkle in his eye. He was also highly intelligent, but just couldn't sit still for long or short periods of time. He was very funny and I thought he was a gifted child with a lot of energy. I liked the kid, but other counselors were just annoyed with him and wanted him to fit into their idea of an easy camper. Complaints were made to his parents, and for the last month of camp, he was put on some drug to help calm and sedate him. It was truly heartbreaking. The child came to camp like a zombie each day thereafter and left like one. It was as if they had sent a different child. His zest for life, his spunk, his sense of humor were all gone. It was truly a tragedy. But the other counselors were happy. How selfish. I hope that he was taken off of the drug and wherever he is now, that he is a happy and creative individual, full of his awesome energy, even if it is a bit over the top.

We must think deeply about what is best for our child, not for us. If our child is like the boy I mentioned and has a lot of energy, then why not get him involved in sports, or have him play outside after school to work his energy off. It might take a bit more effort from us, but to drug our child so that we have peace is the epitome of selfishness and is reprehensible to me. I'd like to add, that there are some parents who just believe what they are told by their MD or other credentialed advisor, and are not selfish, but misguided.

PRAISE

Be careful what you praise or laugh at, as the message to your child is simply, "Do that again, it's good." I recall having the kids sit at our new piano that I bought for fifty dollars from our local community theatre. Ira and a large male friend of ours, Lare Garza moved it to our home and just barely. Finally through the door and firmly planted in its new space, the kids excitedly sat and played it for the first time. I was so happy to see them sitting together nicely at the piano, and plucking away at the keys, that I just grinned a wide grin and praised their playing beyond what they may have needed. It wasn't that I expected them to be good, and admittedly they were at times pounding the keys and my eye was even twitching a little as it was so very loud. Lare looked at me and said, "Why do you keep telling them good job, if you don't like the volume?" I thought, well because they are playing, and sitting together without a fight. But he was absolutely wise in his words. I should have told them, "I'm so happy to see you sitting so nicely together and playing, but if you press the keys with less force, I'll bet it will sound even better". And of course, my eye would stop twitching.

It made me realize that our praise, praise, praise culture is out of control. "Great Job, Jake! Way to go Leah!" Are we even paying attention to what the children are doing? I know none of you would do this…. must just be me. But is it? I bet we are all guilty of going into forward praise mode and repeat. Since that day I strive to really see what they are doing that I am praising or smiling at, as very often I will find something they do to be extremely funny and will smile and possibly laugh. Unfortunately, the laughter evoking antic may also be a delinquent behavior that should be ignored or even at times, corrected. We are not to be their friends first, but parents. When Josh tells me, "You stop talking mommy". That's when I know that I am on the right track and being a good parent. He would love free reign to rule the roost and wreak havoc here, but I don't want a "Lord of the Flies" on my hands, and so though I believe praise is Very important, I stress focus on the awareness of what it is that we are heartily praising and then proceed or cease my adulation.

There is another form of praise which is simple and only takes about ten minutes of your entire life, but its impact can last for years. It is picture framing. I enjoy framing pictures they have made. I've decorated our playroom with pictures that they made in school or with us. I frame them and hang them and the kids see them daily, and are reminded of how we value their art, and effort to create it. We also have the refrigerator covered with their homework, poems, art projects and pictures. We rotate the pictures each season and keep them all in the basement in large plastic containers so they will have them when they are grown. I know that they are proud of their art, because they are constantly making me different things and asking which part of the house they will be placed. They feel valued, and its such a simple thing to do, and doesn't interfere with decorating.

The majority of their art is in the playroom where it is a perfect fit. The rest of the art is scattered unobtrusively, not standing out too much, even next to antiques from the 1800s. With a good eye, you can satisfy your child's sense of self, and have a great looking home. And of course, framing photos of them and putting them on the mantle, or hanging them on the wall is another great way to express your love for your child. I have their pictures either hanging or sitting all over the house in a variety of areas. It was also an exciting project to find and then frame each school picture in the five by seven size, placing them in chronological order. It is truly astounding how quickly they grow in one year's time, and having them lined up year by year is fun for everyone to see. However, my favorite thing to do, as well as their favorite thing to notice, is pictures that were taken of them either alone, or with family and friends, that were of particularly fun scenes or events in their lives, and at twelve cents a picture, what do you have to lose.

DISCRETION- WHAT'S THAT?

One of Joshua's more troubling yet simultaneously endearing qualities is his lack of self-monitoring and discretion. I can most certainly credit that trait to Ira as well. I can't begin to tell you how many times I will cringe as Ira speaks his mind about one race of people or another. Don't misunderstand. He is not at all prejudice. He just relates facts of different ethnic groups with great ease, no malice, but still nerve racking. I remember the two of us also in couples counseling one year, pre-children. He was sitting on the couch, and pulled out a Q-tip and starting cleaning his ears in front of the therapist. "See!" I told her. "He doesn't care..." It's not that he doesn't care about me, he just doesn't care about social norms. He will say whatever is on his mind wherever we are, and to whomever we are with, even the kids teachers! I avoid dinners at Hibachi due to the table sharing aspect... And now that Josh is talking, I have two and the same on my hands. Guess God wants to lighten me up and make me less socially aware....

The beautiful part of this trait however, is that I know exactly what is on both of their minds, therefore I never have to guess at what they are thinking. Unfortunately, it's not always very politically correct. I guess I'd hate to be married to some guy who is very secretive and non-communicative, but a middle ground would be nice. I remember the first time Ira came over to my parents house to meet them. Most people are nervous meeting their girlfriends parents. Not Ira. He is handsome and charming, and not insecure. He also has no concept of forbidden ground. So he went over to their refrigerator, looked through it and started pulling items out of it such as French's Yellow Mustard and White Bread. He asked my mom, "What is this?" as he pointed to the two items. "Bread and mustard." she said. "Barely" was Ira's response. She just stared at him like a deer in headlights... He was right though. French's yellow is NOT deli mustard with its mustard seeds and depth of character, but really Ira.....??? Surprised that they still paid for the wedding.

The other night we drove through a beautiful Living Nativity scene at Orchard United Methodist Church. Once a year, volunteers put several hundred candles into large milk cartons, and create a path for cars to drive through and view other volunteer actors dressed as characters of the nativity. They even had animals outside with them, and despite the freezing Michigan temperatures, the volunteers braved the cold, and we drove through. Before we went however, I made sure to have a discussion with Ira about his ability to control his mouth there. I am a new Christian, having been Baptized last year. Ira was not very happy about my choice, and after several months has lightened up. I was afraid that he would say disparaging remarks at every stop on the drive, making fun of the outfits or the concept etc... I spoke with him, letting him know it was very important to me that he doesn't do that, and that I'd rather go alone if he can't control himself. He agreed to behave and so we all went through.

Josh was very excited to see the animals, and kept urging me to pull forward to them, but there was nowhere to go. We had to wait for the cars to move. He absolutely didn't want to pause at the singers who were before the animals. In his mind they simply slowed his progress down to the Alpaca! So as we pulled up to the singers, Josh, not Ira opened his window and screamed "Stop Singing!!!". I turned ten shades of red and locked all the windows from that point on.

I could tell people it was a sensory overload, which it might have been, but I also believe that he just wanted to get to the animals. I felt badly for those singers caroling out in the cold sacrificing their comfort and time to bring some holiday warmth to us as we sat snug in our SUV hot cocoa in hand with the heat to a comfortable eighty-one degrees and butt warmers on high. I hoped that his dyspraxic pronunciation left them clueless as to what he screamed.

After "enjoying" our Nativity drive, we then drove over to a local Greek Diner and our waitress was a bit overweight. Josh was just noticing the surroundings and people and as she walked up to us, he said, "She is big." I thankfully did not hear it and I truly hope she did not either, but Ira and Amalia reported it clearly after she walked away. He wasn't looking to be malevolent or injure her feelings. He was just describing his surroundings and what our waitress looked like. Had I heard him say it, I wonder what my response would have been. Perhaps I will have to start teaching him to monitor what he says, so as to not hurt peoples feelings. How does one explain that to a child with Autism.... Perhaps that will be for another book, once I figure that out...

After his description of the waitress occurred, Ira went to the restroom just as a very elderly woman was escorted into the diner by a man who seemed to be her middle aged son. I said to Joshie, "When I'm old like that, will you help me and take care of me?" He said, "Yeah." Without much affect, but it was still a yes, so I was happy. Josh then became very curious about this elderly woman who was slowly walking towards our part of the restaurant, and he took a liking to her immediately. As she walked nearer to us, supported by her walker, Josh said, "Come sit with us.", which actually sounded more like "Cuh sih wit us" due to his lingering Dyspraxia, speech disorder. He moved over even closer to Amalia, actually making room for the woman who smiled at us, but who also looked slightly confused. Josh then tried to reach out to her to pull her next to him. Thank God he missed her arm, and she kept walking. I said, "He really seemed to take a liking to you." She smiled. Disaster averted.

When we initially sat down at our table he and Amalia decided to sit next to each other. Not always the best thing to allow, as they can start poking each other, or fighting about one thing or the other. Nevertheless, they were so cute, hugging each other as we entered, that I thought okay, why not. Let's give it a try. As they sat down, Josh even put his arm around her. Amalia was very loving back to him, and it was adorable. Particularly charming, as Josh had worn his Spongebob robe over his clothing because we were not planning to eat out, but to simply drive through the nativity scene and return home. Anyhow, there they sat, cuddling and sweet, cozy in his robe. Of course it only took a moment or two more for Amalia to start to feel her personal space infringed upon. Josh sat very close to her, so I said, "Josh, move over please." He did, but in the wrong direction. He moved closer to Amalia instead of further away. He did literally what I asked, but in the wrong direction. I wonder if that was purposeful. Hard to say. I then corrected him and asked him to move away from Amalia so she has more space. He complied. Then they both ordered their customary pancakes and bacon, even for dinner.

I recall the very first years that we started to take Josh to restaurants to help desensitize him to noise, such as dishes clanging, and people talking all at once. There was one time that he just got away from me and ran to a table with some people that he seemed to like, and he actually pushed his way into their booth and just sat down with them. I apologized profusely, but he is so cute and darling that they seemed to like it. Still, allowing Josh to wear a robe out, or sit with someone else for more than a second of my own choosing, is like asking for a problem in the future, as he will then log it in his mind as "Hey, did that, so I can do it again, and will." Next time we go out, I will have to make a stand in the laundry room and make sure the robe stays at home.

Now that Joshua is speaking in sentences and understanding what we are saying, I am finding the most surprising things occur. If any of you have ever watched Star Trek, and know who Spock is from the original series, then you may know where this is going. Josh will take whatever I say literally. I truly mean, whatever. It's surprising to me how many things I've realized that we say in the English language, that don't actually mean what they literally mean. For instance, most people know that the phrase "Take Five" actually means, take a break for five minutes or so. Josh when hearing that phrase looked around for five things to physically pick up or take. The other day we were doing stretching exercises and I said, "Touch the sky!" When he looked frustrated and started stretching towards the sky and trying to expand his body, I realized the misinterpretation.... He earnestly wanted to do what I asked, and touch a cloud up high in the sky.

There are so many obscure instances that this has occurred that I have learned to watch what I say to him. I am especially careful when giving him directions. If I ask him to brush his teeth and get ready for school, I need to specify an order to make it easier for him to follow. "Brush your teeth and get dressed" are two things that he cannot do at the same time, but the phrase sounds as if they are paired together and should be done simultaneously, at least in his mind as well as many others on the spectrum. So, I have learned to say, "Go first to the bathroom and brush your teeth. After you brush your teeth wash the toothbrush off, and then go to your room and put your clothes on". With the order clearly given, and the further description of first and then second delineated, Josh doesn't look at me confused, overwhelmed and stuck.

With the proper phrasing, he understands that he is to first brush his teeth and then to go get dressed. The other more fluid and casual way of asking him to do things often caused him to look stressed out and confused. Over time and repetition of such tasks, I can go back to saying "Go brush your teeth and then (voice emphasis on the word THEN) get dressed please." However, it took many months in the beginning to get him there. Now he enjoys the autonomy of getting himself ready for the day, and is one step closer to becoming a self-sufficient adult. Don't lose faith in what you are doing if you know it is right. Even if you don't see any results at first, or even for a long time, just keep plugging away, and know that in time your work will register.

Self-care was the absolute first on my list of things I intended to help Josh achieve. Well, that and speech of course. I would shudder to think that when Ira and I are gone, Amalia would have to take him on as an adult. That's not fair to her, and I have never really seen him in my fantasy life, not improving. I believe wholeheartedly that he will live a completely normal life, better than normal, and not need any outside help whatsoever.

In the beginning self-care entailed potty training solely. Now that he is older and has achieved that, the list has morphed. If you are in the potty training days, or just flirting with the idea of tackling that task, trust me when I say that it is a huge milestone that will make yours and your child's life far easier than before. Now that Josh is potty trained a milestone has been reached and a huge stressor has been removed from our daily life and has thus freed us up to focus our attention and energy on helping him in other areas.

For many years, we chose to put Josh in shoes that closed with Velcro. It was time consuming to tie shoelaces, and he was so fidgety back then that it was a struggle. Most recently, we bought him some shoes with shoe laces and he is learning to tie them in occupational therapy at his school. The Occupational Therapist, also known as OT has a shoe that they work on, as well as his own that he is wearing. Josh feels more grown up with his big boy shoes on, and waits patiently for us to tie them for him. In fact, he demands we help. "Help!" he orders us each morning as he sits on the laundry room bench with his shoes next to him. As I write this I realize that there really is no reason he can't just put them on himself.

Part of the problem with being an Autism mom seems to be that we overcompensate and sometimes do things for them that they are able to do themselves. Sometimes that's okay, especially when they are sad and overwhelmed, but not at times like this morning, when Josh was perfectly content, smiling, sitting with his shoes and giving me orders. I also have known from the OT's reports that his fine motor skills are advanced. Fine motor deals with small tasks the fingers do such as tying shoes laces or holding a pen to write. Some children on the spectrum have great difficulty with fine motor tasks. Always ask yourself if you're doing too much for your child. Can he do this himself? If so, then why not let him. Practice makes perfect. Start your day earlier and leave time for him to do extra tasks such as tying his own shoes. You are growing him up to be an independent fully functioning human one day. What better gift is there?

PLANNING FOR YOUR CHILD'S FUTURE

Most of us don't want to think about the fact that one day we will not be here for our child or children. In fact, I avoided that thought vehemently, as it was too scary to face, until one day I was called back for a second mammogram. It happens that my results were good, and that the only reason I was called back, was because I had lost so much weight, that the readings didn't make sense to them. I am totally fine, healthy and beyond grateful. Still, there were five days in which I had to wait, many wait longer, to find out my good news. The only reason I got in so quickly was because the scheduling coordinator was empathetic to my pleas as I explained that I had a son with Autism and I was having panic attacks. During those few days between the day of my appointment and the shock of the call back, I spent much time in deep introspection, communion with God, and also at a lawyers office, creating my will, which included such topics as Guardianship, as well as Finances.

It's remarkable how such potentially awful news can really wake you up to what is important in life, and it can also show you who really cares for you. My husband and I thought that we had a large list of people who would agree to care for our children should we both pass. In fact, the reason we never got around to making a will, was that we didn't really want to think about those things, and we just assumed that we would have many good people who would step up. Boy were we wrong. When push comes to shove, and others consider that you might actually be ill and they would have to follow through, then I guess the thought of caring for a child on the spectrum, that isn't theirs, renders the answer of no, at least from some.

I was truly shocked, at the people who declined. I would have said yes to them in a second. But in retrospect, part of my learning curve that week was to separate the wheat from the chaff, and to truly find the very best people to be named in our will as guardians of our children, as well as those who would be in charge of our finances for them should something occur. Again, there's nothing like a potentially bad diagnosis to get you thinking about these topics, and to spur you on to take quick action. In fact, it is the only truly responsible thing to do. As I look back to the time in which we had no will in place, I am astounded that we waited so long, and I feel like as if I was not being a good and responsible parent. My best advice to you is to look it square in the eye now. Ask the tough questions and receive the true answers from your friends and family. Someone I had considered my best friend for almost twenty years said, "Absolutely not, and I can't deal with this now. I'm going to Sweden in two days." Well, so much for fair weather friends...

In the end, I learned about who was compassionate enough to spend more than five minutes of their life talking to me when I thought I was dying, and those who wrote me beautiful letters of hope and inspiration, and promises to me for aid to our children should the results have been sour. I also feel great peace that the proper arrangements have been made should anything happen to either of us. And I am so grateful to the people who stepped up in love and faith, and blessed that our children's future, in the unlikely event, will not be given to some indiscriminate judge to decide.

Because caring for children is such a huge responsibility, it is understandable that someone might decline, and even more understandable that if your child is Autistic, that they might feel truly unequipped and decline for certain. Therefore, I again urge you to discuss this with people and get a Will created, after you find the perfect people to name. In this particular case, Ignorance is definitely Not bliss...

LESS EXPENSIVE IDEAS FOR FUN WITH YOUR CHILD

I realize that throughout this book I have named ideas of activities for you to do with your typical as well as your autistic child, some over-lapping. Not all of them have been easily affordable, such as Bed and Breakfast/Hotel time with your typically functioning child, or trips to resorts with both. Therefore, I have come up with alternative ideas for you to consider. We have done these following things when our budget was excessively tight, and they proved just as successful.

In lieu of a retreat to a Bed and Breakfast or a Hotel, I in the past would take Amalia out early in the morning, waking her even before Josh was up, so that it would seem as if she was not with him the entire day, and start at a local Starbucks, enjoying one of their special drinks, and playing UNO with the UNO cards that I brought with us, which you can even find at a Dollar store, for yes, only one dollar! We would then walk around the city we were in, feigning a nature hike, looking at different things such as birds in a park, or finding neat things in shop windows. If the weather is inclement, then a mall is another option instead of the great outdoors. We spent many fun girl days walking around a local mall, exploring different shops, and even creating lists of things that we would like to get another time, either for ourselves, or for loved ones. Lunch can be a local Taco Bell, or other inexpensive place. It doesn't matter where you eat, just as long as you're together, and you're not checking your Facebook page as you sit with your child. Give your full attention to your sweetie. It really does make a difference for the good. Next Amalia and I would do a drop by at a friend or relatives home for a couple of hours, then eventually we would have dinner and return home, after Josh was in bed. It was a long day to be sure, but it was fruitful in that she enjoyed my full attention, no Josh to interfere and take over as he does so well.

When Ira and I lived in New York pre-children, he was making very little money in the record business. I remember taking CD's and listing them on E-bay for ten dollars each, then walking them over to the post office to ship them each week. We literally ate rice and beans off of that money for quite sometime. His father owned our apartment, but we still had rent to pay, and not much to cover it. It was a very tight time financially. In fact, I remember Ira sending his dad the rent money a few days late one month, and I received an eviction notice the next week from one of his lawyers. I guess they expected me to pay, but I was pregnant and not working at the time. Nonetheless, I really do understand what it is like to live paycheck to paycheck.

The final straw, and reason I was able to leave New York occurred one spring afternoon. Ira loved working at the record store, receiving promos, going to concerts, soaking up all the information he could about a variety of music. In fact, he pretty much wrote a book on world music that one of his customers continually drained him of information for. When he came home I would make it a habit to go to the backyard of our apartment building for some alone time and fresh air. It was truly a hidden paradise in New York, spanning two full blocks and housing play structures, a large grassy area with picnic benches, a basketball court and small walkways for privacy in nature, well, as natural as you can get surrounded by skyscraper apartment buildings. In the evenings thousands of fireflies lit the grassy area and it really did feel magical. Many of our beloved pets were even laid to rest back there. Where else are you to bury a bird, gecko or fish in Manhattan? There was even a security guard there so only residents could use the backyard. It was my escape and breathing space when I could no longer handle living in 580 square feet of space, virtually one room, with a husband and two babies who would wake each other up one after the other.

My neighbor and British friend Maria who also had a toddler, saw me crying in the back and sat with me. She too had been in a similar predicament, being a foreigner and married to a New Yorker who could not yet provide her and her daughter with a decent sized home. I really felt in that defining moment in our backyard, that if I didn't get us out of the apartment, that I just might die and I told her so.

My father in law had us looking at one apartment or the other, kindly promising to buy one that we liked as he could easily afford to do so and said that he wanted to. In fact, I had looked at about twenty apartments that he said he wanted to buy for us, over a two year span, but it never panned out. As soon as the papers were to be signed, he canceled. I smile recalling the time that I offered 1.8 million of his dollars at his command, for a four bedroom two floor apartment in the same building. Ironically, I didn't have eighteen dollars to my name at the time. I was so hopeful and naive. I was so abundantly grateful and excited, but alas, Dad-in-law had yet another change of heart. So after two years of being on that roller coaster, I decided in the backyard with Maria's encouragement, that to Michigan I must go. I told Ira later that day, and mailed my parents one box of our things via UPS. There went my last eighteen dollars, but it was money well spent. I kept selling CD's and sending more boxes, until one day we had very little left in our apartment number 7F, and in a horrible fight, I demanded we leave for my parents. Ira acquiesced, as he realized that no other solution was in sight and that I had tried it his way for far too long. I would highly advise not leaving New York to drive through the mountains of Pennsylvania at 7pm. Wait until the morning when visibility is better and when tensions are less.

We spent ten days at my parents home and I found us an apartment that was double the space of 7F, nicer, WITH a washer and dryer, no nanny's hogging all eight washers to contend with in a basement laundry room, and I even painted the kids room a lime green! We did it, and it was truly the best thing that could have happened for us all. In fact, I am grateful to HD for not coming through on any of the NY apartments. I can't even imagine living in one of those cramped "Luxury" spaces. It astounds me in retrospect that people pay as much as they do there. Our 580 square foot studio is worth more than the 4800 square foot house we now inhabit. Guess it's all about living in the city... Still, I was one of those double stroller pushing, latte carrying, cell phone shouldered, Fairway grocery bag rack mom's - just pushing through. No wonder they say New Yorker's are tough. You Have to be...

CARE FOR THE CAREGIVER

Several years ago, when both kids were babies, I had a kind friend, David Andrew Macdonald, remind me of the airplane face mask analogy. He said, "Even on airplanes, parents are encouraged to take care to put masks on themselves first, and then to equip their child with the life-saving device." He said, "You can't give away what you don't have." I thought it a selfish idea and just appreciated that another human being could empathize with me, but I didn't actually employ his advice, at the time. I continued on automatic pilot, trusting no one but myself to care for the kids, I did absolutely nothing for myself, but once a week I would wake up early, approximately five am, to go alone to Starbucks, leaving the kids and Ira asleep at home. I did this, because I knew that they would sleep until at least seven am, and so I could enjoy about two hours of uninterrupted latte and book time for myself and myself alone. In retrospect, this was still a good idea, but wow was I a bit of a control freak. I think that any good mother is on some level, but had I cared for myself more, I believe wholeheartedly, that I could have been an even better mother.

As many new mothers do, I also made the mistake of cleaning things whilst they napped. I could have taken a shower, painted my nails, read a book, but no. Their naps became chore time for me, so when they awoke, I was not refreshed. I may have even napped with them if I were wiser back then.

But that was then, and this is now, and oh what a difference there is. Bela knows all of Josh's idiosyncrasies and is gentle and loving. She was with us when he couldn't speak a word, nor could he appropriately respond with head gestures such as yes or no. He just couldn't communicate at all.

She has become like a part of our family, and at least twice a week, she gives us much needed respite as I described before. Both of the kids love her. She is also very sensitive to Amalia, and does not allow Josh to hog the limelight, and so Ira and I take a break, whether it be a movie, a local diner, or when funds were low, we'd just sit at Starbucks or walk a mall or park. I reiterate this point to remind you to care for yourself and to find a good caregiver for the kids to give you the chance to rejuvenate. There is always something you can find to do that takes you away from Autism enmeshment, and it is also very healthy for a marriage to have a date night or day each week. Let's face it. The divorce rate is super high. If you cannot find a good babysitter, one whom you truly trust, who is teachable, and sincere, kind and empathic, but able to set rules, or you just don't yet feel comfortable leaving your kids with someone, or cant afford to, then make sure that once you get your kids to bed, that you spend time with your spouse in a special way.

Light a candle, watch a favorite show, eat some new foods, just try and make it a different and special time for two, and yes, even if you're exhausted... In our small New York apartment, we didn't even have a kitchen table. I bought an outdoor mosaic tiled table and put it by our window which sort of kind of had a view of the Hudson river, if you crank your neck. Trump built a bunch of buildings there which ruined it for us, but we would sit at that small mosaic table, and I would buy a single rose, and put French cafe music on, and pretend that we were in France where we were engaged. It is still one of 7F's more fond memories.

I remember our engagement in Carnac very clearly. I of course wanted to go to Mont St. Michel, Paris, Versailles and all of the more common places that you hear about in France. Not Ira. After visiting my choices, he decided that we would take a road off the beaten path and go to a small town called Carnac, France, in Brittany. Carnac has fields of ancient Megaliths and Dolmens similar to the ones scattered about England such as Stonehenge. They are still unsure as to what purpose these large rocks served, but they are still standing, thousands of years later. Ira had it in mind to propose to me there under one of the ancient Megaliths.

What he did not expect, was that when we arrived in Carnac, Mid-March, that tourist season had not started, and it was cold. Thus many restaurants were closed and transportation was difficult to find. So after eating at the only open restaurant there, and avoiding the eyes that were left on the shrimp they served, we had to walk back to the hotel in the cold as we could not find a ride. On the way, I was noticing his nice behind, and decided to run over and grab it, but as I did so, I twisted my ankle, quite badly on the curb and could not get up. Fortunately, a nice couple in a black Mercedes pulled over thinking that Ira was assaulting me, and I spoke to them in French explaining our situation and they drove us to the Hotel Carnac.

The next day, proposal day, Ira spent half of it at the local pharmacy bringing notes back and forth to me and the pharmacist, written in French which ultimately helped the pharmacist discern exactly what I needed, wheel chair included. That evening Ira looked nervous as he was dressing and redressing for dinner. He finally settled on an outfit that really didn't match at all and looked strange. In fact, he looked like he was ill, but we made it to a field with Megaliths and after pushing me out into the lentil field which smelled like feces, he knelt down on my wheel chair foot and asked me to marry him. I of course said yes, and voila, we were engaged. There is a picture of me holding up my hand with the engagement ring on it, and looking slightly special myself in that chair. Ah, young love...

So engaged we became in Carnac, France. We spent the very next day at a local museum that Ira really wanted to peruse. The people were so kind to him for taking me through on a wheel chair, as if he was such a hero. Little did they know... As Ira was pushing me past a display case with ancient skulls that attracted him, he screamed, "Look at that skull!!!" He then let go of my wheel chair, and ran without a second thought, to the skull case. As he let go of me, I continued forward in unstoppable wheel chair and ultimately crashed into another display case housing ancient jewelry. Fortunately it did not fall over, but wobbled enough to scare me. He was so pleased to see the skull, that he was totally oblivious to my plight. Warning warning.....

This type of fascination with items that most people do not find as exciting is very typical of the Autistic spectrum individual. Josh had a phase where he spent hours lining trains up to his perfect specifications.

The next day we were to leave beautiful Carnac for Paris again. We were running a bit late due to my injury, but made it there in time for boarding. Unfortunately, there was no plank to help me get on board the train, and it left precisely on time, with me still climbing on, legs dangling, and passengers sending me the most hideously pitiful looks you would ever hate to have. That was the last I saw of Carnac. Maybe one day we'll take the kids there. They were a kind Bretagne people and it was a very quaint and ancient village with cobblestone streets. Lovely. Pity however, is something I have never enjoyed. Some people seem to thrive on it, but it is honestly sickening to me, and feeling it at the restaurants with Josh, or on the train due to my previous injury, has set a fire inside of me to not be pitiable. Compassion from people is great, but don't get stuck into a pity party state. It will only serve to tear you down, never build you up.

Vacations to France are a thing of the past, but in order to have some escape, I still rise early each day and enjoy the quiet. It keeps me sane. If you're not the early rising type, I have another idea that you might like which reminds me of a commercial I heard in the 1980's. When things get really stressful, then don't feel like a failure if you need your spouse to take over. Go into your bathroom, and let "Calgon" take you away. Make a bubble bath, read a far away mind expanding novel, relax and return refreshed, renewed and better for everyone. I used to do that and hear the kids yelling downstairs, and it really seemed to ruin my peace and the break felt more stressful than had I stayed there "on duty". You just have to get to a place of trust, if you're anything like me, and let your spouse know that if there is an emergency to come get you, but otherwise to let you have your hour in peace. If you state that pre-respite, then hearing various noises downstairs shouldn't unnerve you too much and you will know that if there really was a real problem, that he or she would come and get you, so worrying is truly fruitless.

DOCTOR'S VISITS

If your child's autism was triggered by vaccinations, as in the case of our Joshua, then trips to the doctor's office can be incredibly anxiety provoking. I practically walked into their appointments in pre-panic attack mode for several years, as I was so reminded of what had happened in the supposed place of help. I'm not writing this to blame anyone or to villainize the doctors or modern medicine. I am simply telling you exactly the truth of what happened to Us. Twelve hours after the Measles Mumps and Rubella shot, Josh developed a rash on his chest, started shaking his head back and forth, stopped making eye contact and started to spend a lot of time staring at the ceiling and fans, not us.

I think that doctors are just doing what they are trained to do, and since they listen to scientific reports and there haven't been many that have been publicized which prove that vaccines are harmful, (though they do exist) then they just continue about their business, in the hope that they are preventing children from becoming diseased and epidemics from spreading.

So, if you have a similar story to ours, then you may appreciate this advice. We switched doctor's offices and chose to see the son of my childhood pediatrician, now a doctor himself. It was an annual exam for Josh, and of course, they didn't know our story yet, and expected it to be a vaccination day. Many people believe that they have to do what a doctor tells them to do. This is entirely false. A doctor is your employee whom you are paying. No, you can't pay him to prescribe medication you'd like, I don't mean it like that. You can't request diagnosis or medicines, but you Can completely reject them. Therein lies the difference.

Doctor Bobby as we fondly call him, didn't know who was in his office that first visit. When it came time for me to tell him we are rejecting any more vaccinations for either of our children, he of course, as most physicians do, put up a small battle. I knew however, that the vaccination was responsible for triggering Joshua's autism, so there was no way I would allow it. I was nervous, and I don't like confrontation, but stated calmly and succinctly, that I would be happy to schedule an appointment with him on his time, in his office without any kids around to discuss this issue, but that there will never be another vaccination put into this child's body, ever or his sister's for that matter. If he didn't want to see us as his patient again, he could let us know. I think he got my point, and its been years since that visit, and they have been good ones.

Doctor Bobby even called us, out of all of his hundreds of patients, to give us his own children's former train table and train set. I believe honesty is the best policy with people whom you are afraid of in positions of authority. And it is best to state your expectations immediately, so that they can decide as can you, if you are both the right fit for one another. It is not against the law to deny vaccinations for your children. In fact, I signed a waiver at the kids school stating that they will not have vaccinations for all three reasons that were listed. They had three boxes to check. They were Religion, Medical and Other. It was easy as well. There is a false notion that your child will not be allowed in school or at camps if not vaccinated. Again, untrue. The truth is that you must sign a waiver, in case your child contracts one of the dreaded diseases that the center for disease control believes the shot will prevent. I signed the form and was out of the office within a minute or two, no questions asked. I'm just not willing to take a chance with my children's lives, after what already happened to Joshua due to the vaccination.

Our children also know that they won't be receiving a vaccination, and the office and employees there will not pressure us to have them. It is far less intimidating because I set the boundaries in the beginning. Prior to that day, just the thought of taking my kids through any medical office door was terrifying. If this didn't happen to you and your child was born with Autism, then just be careful, as many children on the spectrum are super sensitive and putting diseases and chemicals into their already sensitive systems seems reckless. Josh just went to Doctor Bobby for a rash on his chest. Our new fabric softener was the culprit. If a fabric softener can do that to his body, imagine what more serious chemicals can do... That's just my two cents.

I also like to use the analogy I heard about a bee sting. One person who is stung by a bee may feel pain, and nothing more. A second person may develop a nasty rash and have other uncomfortable symptoms, and a third person may die. I believe the shot was the trigger for Josh, and thankfully it did not kill him. If a bee sting can kill a person, why wouldn't we consider that a shot full of disease and chemicals would do any less....

PARENT CHILD TIME ALONE

I've talked a lot about the importance of taking getaways or days out with your typically functioning child, so that they can have an "autism break". I have also discussed going out as a family, but have not yet delved into the importance of alone time with your child on the spectrum. As important as it is for the entire family to experience outings together, there is also a lot of stress management that can occur for everyone during those times, mainly due to sibling rivalry in our family in particular. I also have to be constantly aware of both of the children's whereabouts, and simultaneously strive to give equal attention to them, and to at least vaguely speak to my husband. (Another reason dates with spouse are mandatory)...

But there is a beautiful thing that occurs when you go out with your special needs child, just you and he alone. You remember where he used to be and how far he has come. You can see more clearly the strides he has made when all of your attention is on him outside of the house. It is easy to be in the home with your child and to go about your own business, not paying him much attention, even if you had decided to spend time with him. Phones ring, dishes call out for cleaning and by the time your time alone is over, you realize that you spent much of it cleaning the house and paying the bills, not playing with your child. When you're out of the house however, there are so very many safety concerns that your full attention must be on your child.

Certain days are mommy and Joshie days. On one particularly special outing, we drove to a cute little town called Plymouth, Michigan, also home to our very favorite Bed and Breakfast, 932 Penniman. It reminds me of a much smaller, and cleaner New York City. They even have a town center with a sixty year old movie theatre and fountain and according to Ira, the very best restaurants in Michigan. High praise indeed. Josh wanted to walk the city with me so that he could experience the "Walk-Don't Walk" traffic signs.

So we walked for over an hour and he was just as excited at the last sign we crossed, as he was at the first. That meant that I was holding his hand, running with him, hurrying across the street as the backwards countdown makes him go faster (guess my safety lessons were a success from the past). We stopped at window after window to discuss the contents since there were so many Christmas decorations everywhere. This kind of time together is a one hundred percent focus on your child, kind of a time.

We also had to navigate the local Starbucks by first using the bathroom, dealing with the noises and crowds, waiting in line, getting a seat, getting our drinks, drinking them, re-suiting up, and going back outside again. I find that when I am out with him now, I don't feel pity from people as much as I used to. Thinking about those times makes me tear up even now as I write this. Feeling people staring at you and pretty clearly thinking, "Oh wow. That moms got it tough. Wonder what's wrong with him. How sad." Going out when those looks would fly my way, was very difficult. I realized on this outing, that they were far fewer, as Josh is far less autistic in his presentation and mannerisms than he was before. I didn't tear up once this time out. I think that's a first.

I also find that being out alone with him is an excellent way to assess his progress for two reasons. Crowd input, meaning the looks that strangers will give or not give. And two, I can compare what used to be a really traumatic event for him, but is no longer. Waiting in a line at Starbucks used to throw him into complete sensory overload. While I could tell that he was happy to sit down in a corner away from the crowds, he wasn't overwhelmed like he used to be. It was a good day today. So good, that we even ventured into a darling little "paint your own ceramic piece" art studio, Creatopia, where he chose to paint a small girl gnome statuette. It was completely crowded and we barely got a table. The table we did get had about one hundred paint containers on it for half the time we were there as they were too busy to clean it off immediately. Nevertheless, Josh sat patiently, seemed to tune out the noise, and just to focus on painting his gnome. I was so astonished at his progress, that I also took him to eat at a local restaurant where he finished his entire meal, didn't whine or yell one time, and sat beautifully. Progress indeed.

I guess that by the time we had gotten into the car and started driving home, about four hours later, I wasn't even thinking that anything could go wrong, and I asked him if he'd like to go grocery shopping with me, another sensory overload experience in the past. He agreed and we went grocery shopping as well. Josh wanted to sit in the cart and I put him in, but he then decided that he wanted to get out and would be in charge of the cart instead. It was so cute watching him push the cart, eyes barely above the handle, helping to put the groceries in as needed. All went well, and then we got in the checkout line at which time Josh decided to keep bumping me with the cart as he didn't want to be stuck there waiting. I told him to stop and step aside from the cart. He created a huge scene during which I stayed very calm, and warned him that he wouldn't be going on our mini-vacation. He quieted and the disaster was averted. It even shocked me that after such a good day we had any problem at all. As I recall past outings, we were lucky to have one good experience for all of the places we would go. I guess I've gotten spoiled. So grateful.

JOSH-ISM

Josh: "Mommy, can I please go and kick Amalia?"

Me: "No Josh, you can't kick Amalia."

Josh: "Please Mommy, Please Please PLEASE!?!"

It's hard not to laugh at these earnest, yet obnoxious requests and statements, as they are stated in such a pure fashion. When he asked if he could beat his sister, he was facing her ready to charge and truly just waiting for me to say yes. Though he does seem to understand humor at times, he doesn't quite understand when he is being funny. And yet, he asked the same question the next day, as he did remember getting a laugh from it...

NO TWO SNOWFLAKES…

Just as no two snowflakes are alike, neither are any two children. I write this book in the hope that what I have done that has worked for us, will also work for you. I also offer red flag stories of things to beware of, so that you don't make the same mistakes I have made. That said, there are people who may see some improvements over time, and others who may see very little. I still think it is important to try and do everything you possibly can to give your child the best chance possible, even if the improvements are miniscule at first or even in the very rare chance that you never see any difference at all. If you don't try, then you ensure you will not succeed and will later look back with regret of what could have been, had you put more effort into him. The only way success is possible, is with effort and risk.

I understand the fear involved. I used to be afraid to try something else for Josh because I thought it might fail, and we would end up even more disappointed and exhausted than had we just stayed at our status quo. Nevertheless, dare and try something new with your child. Give it your all and see if it makes a difference. Write notes, track progress, believe it will work, don't get discouraged. Celebrate any success you see and always look back and compare the great improvements, no matter how small they are, as they really are great.

I remember celebrating when Josh could shake his head in agreement for yes, or no for no. Granted other kids his age were forming complex paragraphs and could read, but for us, Yes and No was gold! Until he learned to shake his head appropriately we had to guess what he wanted or he would make loud grunting noises usually indicating that we were on the wrong track. Those grunts were very stress invoking for all. How great an improvement a Yes or No nod was for Joshua. Had we dwelled on his inability to speak as other children his age did, then we would have been defeated and stressed out. We even tried teaching him sign-language for awhile. He didn't pick up on that, but many children do. Nowadays he is speaking in full sentences, but I really wonder what would have happened back then if we weren't grateful for his small gains. Perhaps he too would have given up on himself.

Children are extremely sensitive to the moods and attitudes of their parents and elders. We give Josh a lot of positive reinforcement and encouragement, never making him feel badly about himself and his inabilities. Granted there were times when we were frustrated and needed time outs for ourselves, but the pervasive message to Josh was that he rocked and was the very best and capable of anything he wanted to accomplish. No matter how discouraged you feel, don't let your kids hear you speak negative words over and around them. Bite your tongue if you have to. Lock yourself in a bathroom, but never let negative or discouraging words come out of your mouth around them. Yes, I spent many hours talking to other mother's with kids on the spectrum, venting my frustrations solely to them and other close individuals in my life. However, I promised myself and stuck to it that it would be completely taboo to speak anything negative to him, no matter how much he tried my patience. Speaking negative messages to your child and disciplining them are two entirely different categories. Here's what I mean.

Never say things such as: "You're bad, dumb, stupid, incapable, annoying, frustrating" or anything else in that realm. If you are feeling like your kid is dumb and incapable and completely frustrating to you, then you need a break. Go to a different room and breathe deeply. Say positive things in your mind about him, thank God that he is alive and healthy and ask for spiritual assistance. If your child is exhibiting an annoying behavior such as repeating the same request over and again, then simply tell him, "I understand you would like to go to the park right now, but we cannot go right now. We will go another day. Let's play with the play-doh instead" If he keeps asking, just repeat what you said. If this continues and it is his fifth request, then tell him. "I already told you that we are not going there today. Don't ask again." Make sure to offer him a different alternative activity engaging him fully so that he can let his disappointment go and become so absorbed in whatever new activity he is doing, that he won't even think of it.

I have found that at times I can tell Josh things such as, "I feel sad when you say "Go Away Mommy." Can you please tell me instead, "I want alone time." There are so many ways to phrase your disappointments in a psychologically healthy manner so that you don't have to become your child's beating cushion, and so that he doesn't get away with speaking badly or behaving unbecomingly.

There is a mother of a now teenage boy on the spectrum, who is so used to catering to her son's every whim, and not disciplining him due to her guilt that he is not well, that she still allows him to climb on her back. He is about 12 years old and will claw her neck so fiercely that she has deep wounds. As absurd as that sounds to some people who wonder how could she possibly allow that? Just wait. If you have a son or daughter on the spectrum, it can become very easy to slide into their personal servant role, feeling so badly for them that you wish to make anything good for them that you can. Okay, I never would allow Josh to claw my neck, nor would he thankfully, but I have sat in twisted ways in a chair, hurting myself to make him comfortable as he sat with me. Remember, we are their parents, and often it isn't Autism, but Bratism that we are dealing with.

Many of these beautiful children know it as well, and Josh will often play on the love I have for him to get me to give him his way. I would call him the Master of Manipulators. He knows how much we love him and will often just give a forlorn look to try and convince and persuade me to grant him his every desire.

I have often purchased him things on e-bay that he really wants. He has seen me do this on my cell phone and whenever he wants something will try and coax me into just typing on my phone and having it delivered. In the beginning of this learning curve for both of us, he expected the toy to just magically appear. It took several purchases later for Josh to start to understand lag time, and for me to finally realize that I could use this as a lesson on the United States Postal Service and thus explain to him that once items are paid for that they must then be wrapped, boxed up, driven to a post office, flown on an airplane, put on another truck and delivered to our door. This lesson has helped him immensely.

Just imagine being a child again, not knowing how things work. Now when he asks about his newest item I can tell him that it just got off of the truck and will be put on a plane which is due to arrive in four days. He understands this, and having tracking information is also useful, though truthfully I just wing it, guessing it's on the airplane and throwing out a number of days over the time I think it will take. He wouldn't have understood any of this a few years ago, and perhaps your child doesn't yet comprehend these types of concepts, but the more you explain things in a step by step fashion, the sooner he will understand better, even if he can't let you know he does. Understanding things gives the child peace, eliminating worry and stress and just plain ignorance. Ignorance is not bliss in this circumstance either. Help your child to understand life processes with repetition, which is the key to learning anything at all.

LET'S GO TO THE MOVIES

After fourteen years of not having a solo vacation, Ira told me I must go. That was exactly what I needed to hear, to relieve my guilty feelings of deciding to leave my babies for more than a day. My parents were scheduled to go on a cruise, and time alone with them has been rare most of my life, both as a child and as an adult. It used to be my three siblings who would steal the attention away, but then it became my own precious kids. Don't misunderstand me. I am very pleased that my parents love to spend time with them, and very grateful that they love their grandparents so much, but that left me with very little alone time at all with either parent.

Well, that changed rather rapidly! My parents cruise was only one and a half weeks away, and within a matter of two hours, I heard in prayer that I should go with them, that this was the chance of a lifetime, especially considering that they have both battled with cancer and won, but are not getting any younger. I felt like this was a once in a lifetime chance to bond with them. I took this idea to Ira who told me I must go. Then I called an indiscriminate travel agency, the first one to come up on my blackberry Google page, and next thing I know, I am delightedly running around, praising God for giving me such an idea, and such a trip! I booked it on the spot, and proceeded, about nine days prior to departure, to pack my entire suitcase. I guess it was time for me to get away. The kids were fine with it. Perhaps my over-mothering nature had worn on them a bit, and they could tell it was important for me to venture out for a week.

The next day I looked up the cruise tours and decided that I would check something else off of my bucket list, and swim with dolphins for a few hours. In shallow water of course, and at a very beautiful and seemingly

102

safe location, Atlantis, on Paradise Island. Being as cautious of a person that I am, I felt like I had signed up for sky diving, and that it was just what I needed to bring some life back to ME, and to live for myself for a day, in the most unorthodox fashion. It was an amazing experience and I still laugh recalling the group of five New Yorkers that I met, and with whom I bonded so quickly, to enjoy such a morning and call ourselves family, but of course, to never meet again. As we approached the wet suit area together, we all started laughing simultaneously at the realization that we would have to fit into them. Two of my NY friends were a bit on the heavy side, and after many a self-deprecating joke they began their squirm into the suits, only for me to realize And have to inform them, that after twenty minutes of their battle getting into the suits, that they had both put them on backwards!!! It only got more ridiculous from that point on and the laughter ensued. I would highly recommend that if you consider swimming with the dolphins, that you opt for the baby, not the parent. I was completely shocked to see how large the dolphins are up close. When the mother of our baby dolphin started to approach us, in shark-like form, my New York friends could see the terror on my face because I was the one petting her baby. They said, "Princess, it's probably your neon pink shoes she's after!" I backed up quickly to the wall. What a fantastic time!

Before I left, I wrote books of notes for both Ira, Joshua's teacher, our faithful babysitter Bela and my brother Mike was also called to be "On call" should he be needed. I asked Bela to stay with the kids five of the seven days, so that Ira would not be too stressed out. I then prayed a lot and got into a Faith-filled place that it would all be fine, as it was divinely set-up after all, since it came to me in prayer and everything went so effortlessly. I very fortunately was correct.

It turns out that time away from the family was not only amazing, invigorating, rejuvenating and relaxing for me, but they also fared VERY well. Here's what ensued.

While I was away, Ira began allowing both kids into his man cave which has a fifty inch surround sound plasma television in it, that occupies much of the small cave. When I am around it is an off-limits, "no kids" zone, because he also has instruments, CDs and DVD's all over and it doesn't seem like the safest room, being right next to the furnace, only a wall away. Nonetheless, he was in charge that week, and decided that it was time to have a Star Wars viewing... Not just "A New Hope, Episode 4, 1977", viewing, but ALL of them. For six of the seven days I was away, he played one Star Wars episode a night, in part to teach them about Star Wars, but also to make the time go by faster. Ira writes science fiction and loves Star

Wars, but I think his motivation was more directly related to the movie making two hours of their afternoon fly by.

Each time our ship would come into a port, I would call and or check my e-mails, as Ira, Bela and Miss Cathy had all promised to update me. I think the funniest e-mail I read, and the most exciting, was that they had watched the 1977 Star Wars movie, and at the very end of the show, Joshie screamed, "We Won!". Now if that isn't complex thinking, I don't know what is. For him, it was a breakthrough. Thus began our movie nights upon my return.

I decided that Ira's cave wasn't so dangerous after all, since they had braved it and survived without my supervision, so I asked to watch all of the episodes as a family in there. The kids were ecstatic and shocked. I believe they thought that I was going to be upset that they had snuck into there, with daddy's permission of course, but if that 's where the flow was flowing, then I decided to go with it and see where it would lead. Josh has watched Spongebob Squarepants for a long time, and other shows such as Thomas the Train when he was younger, but a full movie seemed impossible. It felt impossible particularly due to my previous attempts to bring him to sensory friendly films that the local AMC theatres were kind enough to offer once a month. In a sensory friendly viewing the lights are dimmed, not completely shut off, and the volume of the movie is turned down so as not to disturb the children as much.

I recall taking Joshua alone to a sensory friendly film that he sat down at for only a full two minutes of its entirety. Actually, I gave up after one hour of what seemed like an intense workout. Josh kept running up and down the steps, and then towards the door. He must have been five years old at the time, and with such joie de vie that I didn't have the heart to discipline him. I just kept following him, and running as he got faster and made it to the door which he opened mischievously and then held shut so as to keep me from following... We played this game whilst the other children there either sat rocking with headsets on, or making very loud noises typical of severely autistic children. Josh was the only child playing and running around during the film, which made me feel both grateful, because he seemed more connected than most children on the spectrum, as he flashed his cute little smile at me and then ran away. I also felt exhausted, and concerned that my non-disciplinary stance would create in him a mischievous sprite, but there were many circles of communication happening, and at that point in his development I felt it more important to encourage socialization, than to discipline him. And so it went on, and on, and on, for about an hour until I was simply too exhausted to continue, and worried that he would actually out run me. So we left. I didn't really enjoy that time, and didn't want to repeat it any time soon, and so until I returned from the cruise to find that he was able to sit through an actual movie, we did not venture forth to any theatres whatsoever.

The kids second Star Wars six day viewing was also a success, enjoyed by all with popcorn and Star Wars Gummies, so in another prayer session, as I asked God where Ira and I should go on our day-off time from the kids, with Bela there to watch them, I was surprised, but not shocked to hear that I was to forego part of our grown-up alone time that day, to take the kids, AND Bela to a movie at 3:30 pm, still during the time that Bela was on. I quickly Googled local theatres and since Amalia had been asking to see the Lego movie, I honed in on that, but there was not a 3:30 showing, and I kept feeling as if I was to only go to a 3:30 show for some unknown reason. Since I have been very blessed to follow that voice, I kept looking and there was a movie called, "Nut Job" at 3:30pm, precisely. It happened to be an older film and so there were far fewer showings of it, which probably meant that it wouldn't be as busy. Bela was totally up for the idea, and so we all went to the movies. As we got to the ticket window, Josh told the man selling the tickets, "Don't kick me out." I figured that the support of the man in uniform would be helpful, and with my eyes, and a shake of my head, I urged him to tell Josh the rules. He told him that if he was quiet and stayed in his seat that he would be able to stay. That was exactly what Bela and I had been mentioning to him. We got our customary popcorn and one candy, Junior Mints, Amalia's choice, and thus Joshua's as well, and proceeded to the theatre.

We entered to see only two people. There was a man with his son, who was about Joshua's age, and who clearly had Down's Syndrome. I felt relief upon seeing them, because I knew that if Joshua had any kind of issues, that they would understand. I said as much and we all exchanged comforting and knowing looks and even chatted about the Miracle League programs around town which allow special needs kids to play on a baseball team once a week over the summer. Oddly enough, the only other two people to enter, was a mother and her daughter who had some other kind of special needs issue. I began to wonder if that show was set aside as a sensory friendly show, but it was not. We asked them to lower the sound nonetheless, as Josh rejected the ear plugs I had brought with me, just in case. We all sat there nicely, and ironically, the only people "in trouble" were Bela and I. I had leaned over across Josh to tell Bela something, and Josh put his finger to his lips and spit out "SHHHHH, No talking mommy". He also did that to Bela. It was priceless. He sat through the entire film, not needing to go out with Bela even once.

Having her there to flank him made all the difference and I believe it made it a successful venture because I was not nearly as stressed out as I would have been if I felt all the pressure was solely on me.

We enjoyed a wonderful family outing, and will make trips to the movies a more common occurrence now that we have lived through a successful venture. Josh has a list of shows he would like to see, and I realized that this would not have happened had I stayed home and missed out on the vacation of a lifetime. Sometimes other people can have a really positive influence on your kids, just because they do things so differently. I also learned that Ira is completely capable of getting up on time to get the kids fed, dressed and on their buses. That is a huge relief to me, and something that I didn't believe possible until now. Even Josh was surprised that it worked out. As we exited the theatre he very proudly told the usher, "I didn't get kicked out". Poor kid. Maybe I need never tell him that is a possibility again. On the other hand, it worked...

PRAYER

I am now a baby Christian, and prayer is now a large part of my daily routine. However, the principal of prayer can be applied to anyone who wishes to benefit from it for themselves, their families and the world and you need not be a Christian to apply. At the Very least, prayer can help you to hear what your deepest most heartfelt concerns are, and to realize that certain small or large issues exist that without quiet contemplation, you may have ignored. At its best, it is life changing in the most wonderful and profound ways.

At the start of our journey through Autism with Joshua, I did not pray, except on occasion, such as in childbirth, and it was mostly a "Please God Make this Stop!" kind of a haphazard scream. I also have recently re-read old journal entries that have prayers written once in a blue moon for help with serious issues. And I also recall moments where I would cry out rather angrily and doubt that anyone was even listening to me, but nonetheless I would ask for help for our family and my precious boy.

Years later, as an avid prayer, I have learned that in addition to realizing things that I may have previously ignored, that there is a Good God who loves and listens to us and often times makes miracles happen.

One small miracle occurred not too long ago. I was praying in my head that Josh would eat more protein. Typically Josh will avoid eating much of anything. I believe that due to his stomach issues he is perhaps fearful something will irritate him, and so he avoids eating much of anything other than carbohydrates, unless he is coerced into making some kind of a deal which benefits him, such as a trip to Chuck E. Cheese's, or more time on the Nintendo system which we just hooked up. As I sat on the couch, I prayed to God to help him to please eat some protein, as some people had noted that they thought he was looking too thin. Josh has always been in the 10th percentile for weight, no surprise to me as he is such a finicky eater. When he was in Utero my cravings consisted of salt, spicy food, and pureed salmon, liquified lox were even better. Well, he had been running in my direction towards some toys, but mid-run as I finished my silent prayer request to God, he turned around and ran to the refrigerator, opened the deli drawer, got the ham out and put it onto a plate. I could hardly believe what I was witnessing. He then sat and ate four slices in a row. That was the first time he ever ate any deli meat of his own accord. And, he even got the plate himself.

I also recall praying earnestly that Josh would not kick, hit or try and bite the kind hair dresser that he used to go to. For years Josh has truly abhorred having his hair cut. So much so, that I would actually wait until he was sleeping, sneak into his room with scissors and a small bowl, and trim whatever I could get to. He would oftentimes awake and kick me away. I'd come back the next night to finish. The hair cut would look ridiculous over time, and we eventually decided to go to a professional. We did everything we could do to give him the best odds at a good experience. He even had a television playing in front of him, and was sitting on a motorcycle seat. Nevertheless, total failure, and quite a violent time usually ensued. I literally almost had my fingers cut off as I tried to help the hairdresser. Between the three of us, we could barely manage, but thankfully Josh got out unscathed, except for the psychological trauma and his annoyance with the hair that was on his shoulders until he showered it away. Unfortunately the three of us were a bit beat up.

This occurred every six months for several years, until I realized that I had never prayed for him to have a good haircut. So Ira took him and I prayed the entire time. I had a report that was truly miraculous. Josh didn't even flinch. He sat calmly the entire time as if in a dream. Very surreal. So grateful that I can ask God for anything. Even a peaceful haircut.

I have of course prayed earnestly that Josh would become verbal. For a very long time he did not speak at all, and seemed not to understand what we were saying to him. Over time my prayer was answered. He is now speaking full sentences and understands most everything we say. I am so grateful for his improvements, and also so grateful for my prayer time, because of the ideas and directions that I get from God during those quiet times, which always work out to be the best thing for all concerned, even if I am initially resistant to the instructions.

I'd like to share with you some prayers that I say daily over our entire family, and will insert Josh's name in lieu of leaving it blank. Perhaps they will resonate with you and you will incorporate them. If not, you may find them interesting anyhow. I believe that it is important to arm ourselves daily with God's protection, and so I have adapted the equipping of the Spiritual Armor of God in the following way (these prayers have evolved over about a year's time to the following):

I will start by praying the same prayer, a spiritual equipping of each of us in our family. Sometimes I will do it for someone else who is on my mind. I start first for myself which gives me the energy to continue, then for Ira, Amalia and finally for Joshua in this vein:

Please God Cleanse my Joshua of any un-Godly traits, desires, thoughts, ideas, ways of being, blocks to his progress, obsessions, compulsions, Autism, Dyspraxia, bitterness, resentment, fear, worry, anxiety, doubt, unhealthy attitudes, bratiness, malice or any bad things in or around him. Then please Bless him and Anoint him with your Godliness, Goodness, Healing, Wisdom, Kindness, love, peace, joy, faith, ability to speak, social understanding, intellectual capabilities, the ability to follow you and to be pleasing to you, financial prosperity, discernment, wisdom, and always your eternal protection. Please keep him free from harm, protected on his path wherever he goes each day. Be with him, encourage, love, guard and guide him, and heal him of any blocks, curses, maladies, of anything that plagues him or hinders him in anyway from living the best life you can give to him.

Please bless him with the Helmet of Salvation. Bless his thoughts and ideas to be good, Godly, Wise, Supportive of the very best path you have planned for him, supportive of You, His own highest good, and our families highest good. Please mightily indwell his mind, guarding and guiding his thoughts and ideas for good eternally. May he be a pleasing vessel for you to indwell.

Please also grant him the Breastplate of Righteousness. Bless his heart's desires to be Good, Godly, Wholesome, Loving, Kind, Supportive of his very best path that you have planned for him, Supportive of you, His highest good, and our families highest good. Please indwell his heart mightily, guiding and guarding his desires eternally. May he be a pleasing vessel for you to indwell Eternally.

Holy Spirit, Please mightily indwell and convict Joshua before he says, thinks or does anything whatsoever that is un-Godly, not good, displeasing to you, malevolent, unsupportive of his very best path in life that you have chosen for him, unsupportive of you, his own highest good, or of our families highest good. Please simultaneously show him what he should instead think, say or do that is good, Godly, supportive of his very best path in life, supportive of you, his own highest good, and our families highest good, and further grant him the ability and power to choose and follow through with the good and Godly choice instead.

Bless him further, with your Belt of Truth. Please keep him on your very best path that you have chosen for him, easily, effortlessly, peacefully, joyously, lovingly, kindly, healthily and protectedly, eternally.

Please also bless him with the Sandals of Peace. Grant him perfect peace running through every cell, atom, molecule, and organ of his body, as well as in his spirit and soul. (At this point I have been visualizing everything that I speak, and now I add colors to wash through him. Peace/faith in my visual is represented by a light blue color. I see it permeating every bit of his being as it washes through him, starting at his feet and rising through the top of his head and up and out-OR- it can start in his spirit, expand to his soul, and then through his body) Please further remove anything that is an internal impediment to his peace and faith in you, such as worry, fear, doubt, or anxiety, not to return to him or anyone else. I will sit with this for awhile, really seeing the blue light energy filling him to full and over-flowing until I am certain he is permeated by God's perfect peace, which is equivalent to faith, as worry, fear and doubt cannot exist where there is true faith in good outcomes and God's plan. I ask that he be so filled with your peace/faith energy that no storms can enter or remain within him.

I further request your Godly pink love light energy to fill him full to over-flowing, permeating every bit of him. (Again same thing as before, I see pink light starting at both of his feet and rising through his entire body, bathing him internally and externally with love, and opening his heart in Godly love for God, himself, our family and his friends) Please fill him full to over-flowing with your Godly love light energy. Remove anything incompatible with Godly love, such as fear, doubt, malice, hatred, bitterness, resentment, pride, ego, selfishness, greed, and anything bad, not to return to him, anyone else, or this home.

I also ask that you fill him full to over-flowing with your Godly Green healing light energy, wherever it is needed to fix anything that is not 100 percent in him. (I see an emerald green fill him from his feet on up through the top of his head) Please fix anything within his body, soul, spirit, emotions, mind or anywhere that you see he is not well, or functioning at his best potential. Remove any blocks to his healing, and connect all the synapses in his mind that have not yet connected properly to heal his speech center and help him to speak clearly and understandably. Please remove anything unhealthy or diseased from him, not to return to him, our house or to go to anyone else.

Please also fill him full to over-flowing with your purple-indigo Godly wisdom light energy. (Starting at his feet I see the indigo light of Godly wisdom filling him up his entire body straight through the top of his head) Please always have your Godly wisdom and other Good Godly energies available to him to use, eternally. Please remove anything unwise from him not to return to him, this house or to anyone else.

Father, please bless Josh with your Gold colored Godly light of protection and unconditional love energy. Fill him full to over-flowing with your protection eternally. May it permeate every bit of him, body, soul spirit, emotions, thoughts, desires. Protect him from himself and protect him from others. Always be with him. Please indwell him fully, never to leave him, but always to guide, guard, love, and protect him on the very best path that you have planned for him.

Please Indwell Joshua mightily, and eternally. May he be a pleasing vessel for you to indwell. Never leave him, always be with him to help him.

Please also grant him the Shield of Faith. Protect him with your spiritual shield around his entire being, so that no malevolent energies, darts of doubt, un-Godliness, or anything displeasing to you can touch him, come near him, enter into him or originate within him. And please remove anything whatsoever that is still within him that is displeasing to you, never to return to him, anyone else, or our home.

Please also equip Joshua with the sword of the spirit. Grant him clear speech that is articulated well and understood by all, so that he can speak and be understood. May his words be kind, loving, wise, good, Godly, timely, sensitive, gentle, helpful, supportive of you, his highest self, and our families highest self, intelligent, empathic and blessed by you. I ask all of this in Jesus' name. Amen

I do this every day on each of us, and sometimes it varies. If someone is sick for instance, I will focus my attention with additional prayers for the healing of whatever they have at the time. I can honestly say, that I have noticed a major change for the better since I started doing this many months ago. I even decided to cease doing it and see what happened. Josh had a regression over that time period, and I was not nearly as peaceful and calm when I took a break from this prayer. I felt more anxious and worried, and less trusting that all would be well. Try it. You might find it to be the most beneficial part of this entire book.

Another one I like a lot is:

Please show _____ Your direction and will for his-her life.
Please make _____ worthy, obedient and pleasing to you, walking in your-way.
Please make _____ life bear good fruit and count for good.
Please increase _____in the knowledge of you, God.
Please strengthen _____ with all of your power.
Please help _____ to joyously give thanks, even during difficulties.

And of great value and importance is simple, personal communion with God that is unrestricted. What I mean, is speaking to God plainly what is in your heart, on your mind, troubling you, or praising God for his blessings. No script, no agenda, no prayer request list. This is also an invaluable choice.

In a different spiritual vein, my sister Tova Rachel Citrin who is a practicing Orthodox Jewish woman asked me if we ever buried Joshua's foreskin from his Bris. Ira is Jewish. Don't want to confuse... Noting my God search and seeing my personal dissatisfaction with Judaism, before we married he asked me to promise that we would have a Bris if we ever had a son together. I agreed to the Bris, and he agreed that I would not have to work and could be a stay at home mom. So we had the Bris as agreed, and I am now grateful to be unemployed in the workplace, and full time here.

Thinking over Tova's question, I realized that we never buried Joshua's foreskin. At that time in my life I was truly willing to try anything, even talking to psychics on the telephone. I actually got some good ideas that way as well. Had one woman tell me to start taking pictures of foods you make with him together and then to put them in an album. Not bad. He enjoys cooking and it empowered him to see his successes.

Anyhow, I was determined to first find his foreskin, as Yes, I had kept it. I have great difficulty in even recycling their homework, so it's no surprise that I couldn't just throw away a piece of my babies body. Again, don't judge... Ira had been away in New York for a couple of weeks, and the kids and I went to pick him up from the airport. Little did he know what task was in store for him. Before he went to sit in the front seat he saw a dirt filled Smucker's jar there, which I grabbed as casually as I could, and then asked him to hold for me as I explained how the word foreskin in Hebrew has something to do with the word speech, and my sister told me it must be buried, and before we go home, I'd like him to bury it.

I don't remember him being shocked. I guess after living with me for so many years, he just got used to the unexpected. So he agreed and off to a local park we went. As Ira neared the more foliage filled area, I asked him to please be careful not to go in too deeply, as the forest was filled with tons of Poison Ivy. He humored me and laughed at me teasing me about my overcautious nature... Well, lo and behold, the Smucker's Foreskin Jar was buried, and Ira emerged with Poison Ivy.....

He started scratching immediately, and thought he was going to just get into the car and go home. I told him I'd be back, and drove through the drive-thru at a local pharmacy. I said to the girl. "My son is Autistic, my daughter is a toddler, I'm exhausted, and my husband just got poison ivy after we picked him up from the airport. Can you please help me?" She gladly found the items I needed, so that I didn't even have to go inside with the kids. I paid for them, Ira applied them and home we went. His vacation lasted an additional four days in quarantine. No anticipated break for me. I had to cook his three meals and deliver them to his door. He was so happy he got an extra break, that the poison ivy didn't even phase him. But in the end, the foreskin got buried. So, who knows. Maybe that helped too....

JOURNALING

Having lived through many years of the Autism roller coaster ride, I have learned that journaling throughout them has proved most beneficial. There were many days that I felt extremely overwhelmed, stressed out, depressed, and hopeless. It's not that I have forgotten those days, weeks or months, but living in the present reality, with Joshua fully potty trained for years, behaviors modified, and speech coming at last, I guess I have chosen to focus on the positive side instead of relive the hell that we were living each day. Therefore, what you have read up until this point, is not a full representation of what the years were like for our family or for myself personally. I wasn't always walking around in faith that things would improve, and that our lives would be one hundred percent better. In fact, I was often walking around in a bubble of self-pity and hating myself for feeling pity, over-eating as a coping response, and crying myself to sleep at night. I tell you all this now, in order that you can see that someone else was in your position in many ways, but came out stronger, more patient, less selfish, and with such strong faith that God's plan IS good, that you too can enjoy that future if you just hold on and make it through today.

Here is a journal entry from May 16, 2010, only about four years ago, when Joshua was exactly four and a half years old.

"Needing to vent now. Has been rough with Joshie. A regression of sorts, or just a difficult time. Lots of problem behaviors. Had to leave and get some sanity. He has pushed us all to the edge. Pinching, biting us, hitting and constantly yelling, which is supposed to be good because at least he has an opinion, but imagine living with the perpetual yelling. He must be so frustrated. I love him so much, just wish he was much better. He has

114

come so far, but the aggression probably due to his frustration is tough.

Have decided that he and the family would probably benefit if he was enrolled in summer camp. Please teach him to talk God. I believe in miracles! I believe in miracles! I believe in miracles! I do! I do! I do! Maybe he has been worse because he was sick...? What more can we do for him?

Should I stop the Pro-biotic? No more pizza? Hard core wheat free, gluten free, dairy free, and soy free again? What more can I do? Please advise.....

Please make me a better-great patient mother with him God! Please. I beg of you. Amen. Thank you."

About two weeks later, May 31, 2010, my birthday journal entry regarding Joshua's gains over the past year, May 31, 2009 to May 31, 2010.

"Now for Joshie. He has gained a lot. 1. Eye contact improved 2. Can blow bubbles now which is crucial for speech to come 3. says, "Go" and "Mom" and "Daddy" 4. Understands many simple and complex directions such as "Go get shoes on." 5. Potty trained, mostly "BEST THING EVER" 6. Can wave Hi! 7. Shakes head for yes and no 8. Engages in pretend play by dressing up! He is really improving rapidly this year. We are very pleased and hopeful! I love him so!!!"

If you read the dates, then you must have noted that the two entries were very different. The first entry was full of overwhelming self-pity, sadness and stress, sprinkled with hopeful prayers, and the second of optimism and gratitude only two weeks later. These entries are a direct example of what I mean when I call our experience a roller-coaster ride.

MY HOPE FOR YOU

It is my sincere hope for you the reader that your child of the spectrum improve in a massive way. It is also my fervent prayer that all children on the spectrum everywhere will live in loving homes with parents or caregivers who care for themselves well, and thus have the capability to give of themselves what the child requires, with patience, empathy, kindness, love and faith of the highest possibility. Always believing for an improved future, and celebrating all the successes, even the most minor ones so that their enjoyment and quality of life in the here and now is at its highest possible state.

I am so grateful to God for his guidance and for the whole journey, and I pray that you will all trust in God and follow your intuition, which is his voice manifest in your feelings. You'll know if it is God if it is of a loving nature, and not full of fear, dread, worry or longing. Some of the strangest God given directions have panned out to be life changing in our lives, and most unexpected. If you feel directed to try a new food for your child, or to stop feeding him a certain one, and that feeling doesn't go away, perhaps that is God directing you to healthier choices for him. Who would have thought that a Caribbean cruise would have such a positive impact on our family upon my return. I certainly didn't see that coming. In another vein, if you feel the professionals are wrong, then stand up and walk away. We have so many decisions to make in life, small and large, and they all turn out to be small brush strokes on the canvas of our lives. Why not take some quiet time and consult the master artist, the creator of the entire universe and allow him to guide your brush. He really wants to do just that and certainly can do a far better job than we ever will.

Many blessings,

Michelle Rott Rosenblum MS, MSed

I wrote a song for my children. I feel that it represents how most parents feel about the their kids, and it is something I have sung to them throughout the years

I Love You, You're Perfect!

© Library of Congress: 1-151747851

I Love You, You're Perfect. You're Perfect, I Love you!

Yes, you really are, and yes I do love you.

Your eyes and your nose, your feet and your toes

The smile you wear on your face

The questions you ask, the things that you say…
are perfectly perfect to me.

I love you, you're perfect. You're perfect, I love you.

Yes, you really are, and yes I do love you

Your fingers and hands, the games that you plan

The songs that you sing with such zest!

The hair that you brush, your cheeks when you blush

Are perfectly perfect to me!

I love you, you're perfect! You're Perfect I love you!

Yes, you really are. And yes, I'll always love you!

Whether happy and glad, or angry and mad

I love you just the same.

You are perfectly perfect to me.

ACKNOWLEDGMENTS

Josh did not improve without the help of many. Much appreciation to:

God, Cathy McCotter, Cathy Wiseman, Leah Mattise, Miss Annie, Mr. Mike, Kelly Bowyer, Shawn, Karen, Maria, Monica, Wanda, Susan, Ms. Anne, Magda, Danny, My Parents Sheldon and Carol Rott, Herman David Rosenblum, Doctor Robert Blum, Bela Mittelman, Courtney Pefley, Gina Bryant, Hillary Weiner, Tova Rachel Citrin, Mike Rott, David & Natalie Rott, Jenny McCarthy, The Friendship Circle, Reverend Carol Johns, Linda Hall, Ram Kumar and Snowy, Skylar and Rocky, Ira Rosenblum, and our beautiful daughter Amalia, all of the nameless people who were kind to us wherever we went, and last but never least, Joshua.